100 answers to 100 questions

about

loving your Husband

D0776449

100 answers to 100 questions

about loving your Husband

ask · discover · live smart

Christian
LIFE
A STRANG COMPANY

Most CHRISTIAN LIFE products are available at special quantity discounts for bulk purchase for sales promotions, premiums, fund-raising, and educational needs. For details, write Christian Life, 600 Rinehart Road, Lake Mary, Florida 32746, or telephone (407) 333-0600.

100 Answers to 100 Questions About Loving Your Husband

Published by Christian Life
A Strang Company
600 Rinehart Road
Lake Mary, Florida 32746

www.strang.com

Scripture quotations marked, THE MESSAGE are from, THE MESSAGE: *The Bible in Contemporary English*, copyright © 1993, 1994, 1995, 1996, 2000, 2001, 2002. Used by permission of NavPress Publishing Group.

Scripture quotations marked NAS are from the New American Standard Bible. Copyright © 1960, 1962, 1963, 1968, 1971, 1972, 1973, 1975, 1977, 1995 by the Lockman Foundation. Used by permission. (www.Lockman.org)

Scripture quotations marked NCV are from The Holy Bible, New Century Version. Copyright © 1987, 1988, 1991 by Word Publishing, Dallas, Texas 75039. Used by permission.

Scripture quotations marked NIV are from the Holy Bible, New International Version. Copyright © 1973, 1978, 1984, International Bible Society. Used by permission.

Scripture quotations marked NKJV are from the New King James Version of the Bible. Copyright © 1979, 1980, 1982 by Thomas Nelson, Inc., publishers. Used by permission.

Scripture quotations marked, NLT are from the Holy Bible, New Living Translation, copyright © 1996, 2004. Used by permission of Tyndale House Publishers, Inc., Wheaton, IL 60189. All rights reserved.

Cover design by Whisner Design Group, Tulsa, Oklahoma

Copyright © 2008 by GRQ, Inc.
All rights reserved

ISBN 10:   1-59979-276-1
ISBN 13:   978-1-59979-276-7

BISAC Category: Religion/Christian Life/Love & Marriage

First Edition

08 09 10 11 12—9 8 7 6 5 4 3 2 1

Printed in the United States of America

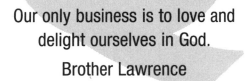

Our only business is to love and
delight ourselves in God.

Brother Lawrence

Contents

Understanding the Differences

Communicating with Him

Keeping It Faithful

Making It Last

Introduction

The relationship between men and women can seem like one of the biggest mysteries in the universe. It seems as if the biggest differences between men and women are not just physical in nature. Men and women think differently, they use logic in different ways, they express themselves differently, and they often show love in different ways. Their physiological and sexual needs are different, and the way they learn is not the same. And just when you might ask how two such different creatures can even get along, you decide to get married and spend the rest of your life trying to understand your husband.

Marriage is a serious undertaking, a unifying of two different people into a cohesive unit. Marriage is the physical picture of the spiritual relationship that God longs to have with you. His goal is that as you learn and grow in your marriage relationship, you will be able to apply those same lessons to your relationship with Him.

Being married is the easy part of the relationship, just as saying you love God is simple. The harder part of the relationship is putting aside your own needs and desires to focus on your husband. Loving your husband is not simply about your feelings—true love extends to wanting the best for him in all things and doing everything you can to make that a reality.

Loving your husband isn't a license for him to take advantage of you. True authority in the marriage relationship comes with a great deal of responsibility. True submission in a marriage is not just about letting him have his own way at your expense. Instead, authority is best learned through submission. As your husband submits his life and will to God, you will be able to lovingly and freely submit to his leadership.

- Love is not just demonstrated in intimate times. Loving your husband can be shown in every aspect of your life. When your desire truly is for the best for your husband in all areas of his life, you will be free to love him into success in all his relationships.

- Keeping God at the center of your marriage and your family will ensure that you are both connected to the One who will carry you through anything.

- Knowing that the success of your marriage isn't all up to you can free you from a lot of responsibility as you trust in God to make this marriage a success.

> *There is no more lovely, friendly or charming relationship, communion or company, than a good marriage.*
>
> Martin Luther
>
> *Hang my locket around your neck, wear my ring on your finger. Love is invincible facing danger and death. Passion laughs at the terrors of hell. The fire of love stops at nothing—it sweeps everything before it. Flood waters can't drown love, torrents of rain can't put it out. Love can't be bought, love can't be sold—it's not to be found in the marketplace.*
>
> Song of Solomon 8:6–7, THE MESSAGE

question

How can you help your husband be the leader in your marriage?

The true leader's first priority is the best interests of the ones being led. Leadership occurs when accountability and authority are combined, resulting in good steward-ship. Your husband's desire to lead his family is a good thing, and you can help him by understanding his decision-making processes, encouraging him when he is down, and helping him stay focused on your joint goals.

answer

In many ways, leadership in a marriage is a lot like white-water rafting. Everyone in the raft has an oar and is told to paddle for all he is worth. There is one person in the rear of the raft who sits higher than the others and can see oncoming obstacles. This person, the sighter, sets the direction for the raft and controls it to some degree with the rudder, while the other rafters propel the raft forward and do the majority of the steering with how they paddle.

As you can see, this gives everyone in the raft a part to play in the success of the ride, and it allows each one to con-tribute to the fun while also creating a sense of responsi-bility. Even though it may seem as though the one sitting up high giving all the commands is getting the easier job, remember that the sighter must remain vigilant at all times, even when the others may relax when the river flows smoothly.

Treating your marriage in this manner will allow you to see that you can share leadership in your marriage without really knowing it. You already play a part in your husband's decision-making processes through your input and through his desire to please you. You influence those around you through your example. Your husband looks good through your accomplishments and your part in his successes.

Leadership in a marriage is not a one-person solo act. It means responsibility and accountability, and it means knowing when to let go of the oars and let the sighter steer.

worth thinking about

▶ **The Bible says** that the best leader must first be a servant, and your desire to share leadership must stem from a greater desire to do what is best for your husband, your marriage, and your family.

▶ **You can lead** invisibly from the sidelines by supporting your husband's decisions and by giving him the information he needs to make good choices.

▶ **The best example** you can set for others is to acknowledge that your husband sets the direction for your family while at the same time sharing leadership with you. Praying together on a regular basis will help establish a foundation of agreement and understanding.

> *Where there is no counsel, the people fall; but in the multitude of counselors there is safety.*
> Proverbs 11:14, NKJV

2

question

Why does he need your respect?

Respect is hard-won and easily lost. Poor decisions, secrets, and unfulfilled promises lead to feelings of disrespect. Your husband associates respect with the core of his being; it defines who he is to others. For your husband, a lack of respect is not simply a difference in opinion, it pervades everything he thinks and does. Your husband needs to know you respect him just as you need to know he loves you.

answer

While your husband may appear to be the strong, silent type, inside he earnestly seeks validation from the people who matter to him. Your respect affirms his worthiness and builds his courage to go out and face the world. Without it, he will experience self-doubt, which will soon manifest itself in all areas of his life.

Understanding that your husband has the best interests of you and your family at heart will encourage you to trust him in his decision-making processes. Offering advice when asked for tells him that you are available when he needs a second opinion or additional input. When you respect your husband, he feels it and is supported and strengthened by it.

The confidence he gains from knowing you respect him will overflow into all areas of his life, including his career, his friendships, your family, and your relationship. You will experience greater levels of all forms of intimacy with him. This newfound confidence will result in better decisions, deeper conversations, and expanded relationships.

Showing respect for your husband will benefit you as much as it does him. You will feel better about your husband in general, and this will create a cycle of more love, more respect, and more trust, resulting in more love. What a wonderful win-win situation!

worth thinking about

▶ **How a man thinks** about himself will determine how he treats others. Encourage your husband every day by identifying at least one good decision he made that day.

▶ **Respect and trust** go hand in hand. Your husband sees your trust of his decisions as a barometer of your respect for him.

▶ **While how your** husband views his accomplishments is important, you can also respect him because of his relationships with you and your children.

This provides a good picture of how each husband is to treat his wife, loving himself in loving her, and how each wife is to honor her husband.
Ephesians 5:33, THE MESSAGE

question

▼

Why is your respect for his decisions so important?

Men tend to view information presented to them as something to be dealt with, either by looking for a solution or by incorporating it into the solution to an existing problem. Making wise decisions, especially as they impact you and your marriage and family, is key to your husband. Your husband looks to you for validation of his decisions because that validation plays an important part in how he perceives himself.

answer

▼

Your husband understands that dissension causes separation, and that is not his goal. He values your input and needs your support to implement his decisions so that you can both benefit from the expected good outcome. The decision is not the most important thing. Agreement between the two of you is.

You can show your desire for agreement by asking questions to assure your understanding of the situation and then gathering information as needed. Allow him to tell you his initial decision before you offer your opinion so as not to sway him. Discussing options together means you each will better understand how the other thinks.

Your husband truly wants to make good decisions, and you can show your respect for him by taking part in the decisions with good grace, by speaking positively about the outcomes, and by encouraging him in his decision-making processes. Commit to learning how to make better decisions together, regardless of the outcomes. A good goal is that decisions be joint decisions, ones that you both can claim ownership of.

worth thinking about

▶ A joint decision will be stronger and more unifying than an individual decision. When you seek your husband's advice before buying a larger ticket item, you are telling him that you value his input.

▶ Few decisions either of you makes will be life-changing; however, allowing hard feelings to creep into your marriage as a result of a bad decision will change the face of your marriage.

▶ Regardless of the outcome of a decision, be willing to discuss with your husband what you both learned and to agree you will continue to work together on making future decisions.

> *When the people of Israel heard about King Solomon's decision, they respected him very much. They saw he had wisdom from God to make the right decisions.*
> 1 Kings 3:28, NCV

4

question

How can you show you care about his self-esteem?

A person's self-esteem, the part that defines worth to oneself and others, can be much like a butterfly—elusive, fleeting, fragile, and beautiful to behold. Even if your husband is the tough macho type, his self-esteem is still easily bruised, quickly diminished, and sometimes difficult to rebuild. Words are an important way in which to tell him that you care how he feels about himself; your actions, however, will speak louder than your words.

answer

Self-esteem isn't only about how your husband thinks about himself; it also relates to his perceptions of how others think about him. Bring out the photo albums to remember and illustrate good family times together. Make plans for another celebration in the near future.

Show him you care how he feels about himself by listening carefully and validating his feelings when he shares his concerns and worries with you. Be sensitive to his need for time alone, and be willing to make time for him when he needs to spend time with you.

Make a point to let him know by your posture that you are attentive to his words. Turn to face him; lean forward; cock your head; look him in the eye. Indicate by your verbal feedback that you understand the importance of what he is saying.

Demonstrate to him in tangible ways that you care about him by showing that you know he is worthy and capable. Trust his decisions, and don't second-guess his motives. Your husband looks for those concrete manifestations of your love and care for him as a person, as a man, and as your husband.

worth thinking about

▶ **Your husband listens** beyond your words and may interpret something by ignoring your words. Make sure your nonverbal communication lines up with what you say and mean.

▶ **Any extra effort** you put into your marriage tells your husband he is important to you. Plan a surprise party for his next birthday or arrange a special weekend away to let him know how much you care.

▶ **Ask if there** is a particular problem or situation that has been bothering your husband for a while. Talk about how you might resolve the situation, and suggest praying together for God's guidance.

> *Whatever is good and perfect comes down to us from God our Father.*
> James 1:17, NLT

question

▼

How can you encourage him to guide rather than control?

There are few things more frustrating than feeling that you are being ordered around without having any input. While everyone would agree it is better to be asked to do something rather than being told, this nicety can get lost within a marriage because of how well you know the other person. Understanding that your husband's desire is to lead and control will help you respond to him positively.

answer

▼

Men want to build and grow, while women want to nurture and expand. Those may sound like complementary goals, but they can often come from opposite points of view. Your husband, in his desire to take the lead, may forget the nurturing and relationship side of the equation and instead go straight into building mode, despite the obstacles.

Your husband's innate desire to lead is part of the way God created him. However, that leadership role is meant to be the result of the combined efforts of you and your husband. He needs you to incorporate his big-picture thinking into your relationship focus so that feelings don't get hurt in the rush to accomplish.

If your husband tends to micromanage, let him know what your schedule is and what your to-do list includes so that he sees you are capable and efficient. Encouraging him to share his schedule with you will develop trust and will let you see if there is any area where you might offer help.

Remembering that God put you together in this marriage to work as a team may take your attention off the outcome and put it back on the process. Suggest he offer you a choice of options to temper his leadership style from controlling to guiding.

worth thinking about

- ▶ **True love** is wanting the best for your husband, putting his needs first, and believing he is doing the same in loving you.

- ▶ **Leadership is about** bringing out the best in others, not about being the boss. Encourage your husband to treat others the way he wants to be treated.

- ▶ **It is usually easier** to follow than to lead. As your husband works through any struggles he has in leadership issues, ask how you can help him.

> *I will instruct you and teach you in the way you should go; I will guide you with My eye.*
> Psalm 32:8, NKJV

Why does he have a different definition of what *clean* is?

How can a young man cleanse his way? By taking heed according to Your word.

Psalm 119:9, NKJV

6 question

Why does he want to make more money than you do?

As husbands and wives seek to establish and understand their roles as spouses, parents, and employees, income can become a power point. Many times, the concept that whoever makes the most money should have control over the household finances is an issue in the marriage. Men have an innate desire to be the leaders of their families, and in many ways they associate their ability to lead with their incomes. Understanding this connection will improve your marriage relationship and will allow you both to realize that money does not define a leader.

answer

When who makes the most money becomes the determining factor of who has control, then your focus is in the wrong place. Leadership is about doing what is best for the family; it is not about income or power. Money is simply a tool to accomplish specific tasks and should be used to meet your family's needs. When you and your husband can view it in this way, you both will be able to separate income from the individual, be satisfied with what you have, and experience true contentment.

Regardless of which of you makes the higher income, be willing to assist your husband in whatever way he needs to make decisions that benefit your marriage. Your husband's commitment to being the leader in your home can be accomplished without considering incomes. Discuss with your husband where he might be willing to delegate some responsibilities while still being the leader in your home. Neither your worth nor your husband's is determined by the size of a paycheck. Your husband's desire to lead is also God's desire for your marriage.

worth thinking about

▶ **Recent studies show** that in the most successful marriages, the husband makes the larger salary, even if the margin is relatively small. This means that if your husband makes more money than you do, it can be good for your marriage.

▶ **Combining family finances** so that all the expenses are paid from your joint incomes can take your focus off each other's financial contribution.

▶ **If you make more** money than your husband, you can reassure him in his position as leader of your family by making sure you don't use your higher income as a weapon, particularly in discussions about money, or when making major financial decisions.

Her husband is known at the city meetings, where he makes decisions as one of the leaders of the land.

Proverbs 31:23, NCV

question

How can you take an interest in his work?

It can be difficult to take an interest in something you don't understand or don't know anything about. The good news is that even if you have little understanding of your husband's job, you can learn enough to be able to talk about it with him or explain it to a friend. Knowing more will enable you to support him in his decision-making process, and will enable you to respond more helpfully when he asks you for advice.

answer

You can learn more about his job by asking pointed questions about his responsibilities, the processes he employs to complete his job, his competitors, and the products or services he provides. In addition, you can do some market research to see where his employer fits into the marketplace, such as reading the business section of the newspaper for up-to-date information concerning his field or industry.

Socializing as a couple with his coworkers is a great way to get to know them without the work environment interfering. Befriending the wives of his male coworkers will build a bridge of friendship. Encourage your husband to include the two of you at work functions where spouses are invited.

Look for ways to promote your husband's business to friends and acquaintances in your circle of influence. Knowing what your husband does will make your husband look good to his managers.

There is a subtle difference between taking an interest in and interfering in his work. Getting those boundaries straight in your mind will allow you to help him when he asks for it. Knowing more about his job will give you another topic of conversation, as well as provide you with insights into your husband's personality and thoughts, which will draw you closer as a couple.

worth thinking about

- ▶ **When your husband** is successful in his job, you will reap the benefits of that success, including having a husband who is happier in his work.

- ▶ **Taking an interest** in your husband's work is a decision for the longer term. Your interest needs to be sincere and not merely temporary or self-serving.

- ▶ **Your desire** to take an interest in what your husband does for a living should be because you want to grow closer to him, understand him better, and share in a significant part of his life that is probably spent apart from you.

> *We don't yet see things clearly. We're squinting in a fog, peering through a mist. But it won't be long before the weather clears and the sun shines bright! We'll see it all then, see it all as clearly as God sees us, knowing him directly just as he knows us!*
>
> 1 Corinthians 13:12, THE MESSAGE

question

▼

How do you encourage him in his job without interfering?

It can be easy to want to put in your two cents' worth when you see someone you love being treated unfairly, especially in an area that is as important as a career. There may be situations where you want to have some input into your husband's job situation, including lack of promotion or recognition, demands on time, and conflicts with coworkers. However, it is important to remember that this is your husband's job, his relationships, and his responsibility to stand up for what is right.

answer

▼

As he works through a situation, wait until he asks for advice before you offer it. Allowing him to come to the solution will empower him in his decision making and demonstrate to him that you trust him. Your husband needs to feel he is in control of his job and career, and stepping in before he asks will cause him to feel he is not able to direct this aspect of his life.

Encouraging your husband to talk through the situation with you is a good way to let him work through the issues.

Don't offer to call in any favors you might have unless he asks. Don't pester him if he seems to be taking an inordinate amount of time working through the situation. Tell him you appreciate him more than his position.

Even if your husband doesn't express any specific feelings of discouragement about his job, he may still have an overall sense of wanting something more. Encourage him by telling him you are proud of him for providing for his family and for going to work when he doesn't always feel like it. Let him know that while you may not completely understand the situation, you are available to help in whatever way he needs.

worth thinking about

▶ **Create an oasis** of safety and calm in your home by having specific times when you will not discuss problems he may be having at work, such as at the dinner table or just before you go to sleep.

▶ **If you perceive** your husband is reluctant to approach a manager, offer to role-play the situation and help him deal with his fears.

▶ **Encourage your husband** to talk to someone outside his employment that he trusts.

> GOD *reward you well for what you've done—*
> *and with a generous bonus besides.*
> Ruth 2:12, THE MESSAGE

question

How can you be supportive of your husband's career choice?

With today's mobile society, it is likely that you and your husband will change careers three or four times and relocate several times as well. Few people stay in the same job or even the same career for more than ten years. You want your husband to feel good about his job and his ability to support you and your family. Your best support will be to appreciate his contribution to your family and the work he does.

answer

The important thing about your husband's career is not what he does for a living, but rather how what he does makes him feel about himself. Since your husband's self-esteem is connected to his job, your attitude toward his career choice is important. If he thinks you do not approve of his work, he may transfer that disapproval to himself as a person and as a man.

You can encourage him in his career choice by assuring him that you are proud of him and who he is as your husband, lover, and friend. Speak positively about the work he does, and how it benefits your family and others.

If you find it difficult to be supportive of your husband's career, it may not be about the job at all, but about the income or benefits your husband receives. If this is the case, consider how you can overcome these feelings without pestering your husband to change careers to suit you. One way to do that is to follow a budget to help reduce spending, which will relieve financial pressures.

Choosing to appreciate your husband and his willingness to work and support your family is an important step. Your attitude will determine how your husband thinks about himself and his job. When he is proud of what he does to support you, he will feel better about himself.

worth thinking about

▶ **Talk to your husband** about his job and the direction his career is taking. Learning more about what he does at work may change your attitude toward his job so that you find it easier to support him.

▶ **If he is thinking** of changing jobs, do some research for alternatives that will combine similar skills and experience he already has.

▶ **Careers can change,** but husbands are forever. Look for positive things to say about his job, even knowing he will likely change jobs in the near future.

> *Let every detail in your lives—words, actions, whatever—be done in the name of the Master, Jesus, thanking God the Father every step of the way.*
> Colossians 3:17, THE MESSAGE

10

How do you encourage him when he is offered another job?

Changing jobs often involves changing employers and locations, and this can be difficult for both of you. Uncertainties about success and his ability to provide for his family will be your husband's main focus; concerns about loss of income and relationships will be yours. Approaching the job offer logically and in unity will go a long way toward encouraging your husband through this time and will help both of you face your concerns together.

answer

One way to address the situation is to look for good reasons to change his job now. Listing them on paper will make them concrete for both of you. This would also be a good time to discuss how you will handle any lack of income between his last paycheck from his current employer and his first paycheck in his new position. List the pros and cons of his current job and the new job, and show logically how both your goals are achieved. Check on housing prices, schools, churches, and other amenities so that your husband doesn't have to deal with this.

Take the focus off you personally and put it onto the benefits of the job offer. Whether you relocate or not, your circle of friends will likely change to some degree. Speaking positively about the changes and how you will incorporate these new relationships into your family situation will free your husband of his concerns about how the decision may impact you and your family.

Your husband may find it difficult to discuss his concerns. Offer your help in making the decision, and then trust that he wants to make the best decision possible. Sometimes the best encouragement will be in your support of him during this process.

worth thinking about

▶ **You can take pressure** off your husband by proactively establishing a budget to accommodate the new income, including concrete plans for any extra money. Seeing tangible benefits of the job change may make the decision that much easier for both of you.

▶ **If you also** work outside the home, do some research on possible job leads for you if you have to move.

▶ **This situation may** open up possible major changes to your lifestyle, allowing you to make decisions you didn't think possible before, such as choosing to stay at home, working part-time, going back to college, or starting your own business. Take advantage of this opportunity.

> *Be completely joined together by having the same kind of thinking and the same purpose.*
> 1 Corinthians 1:10, NCV

How do you handle promotion or job transfer conflicts?

With today's mobile society, few couples expect to work for the same employer or even live in the same town or city for the rest of their lives. Employers have come to expect this mobility, and business thrives on it. Even when the move is a vertical one within the same company, conflicts can arise regarding scheduling, responsibilities, and office locations. Dealing with this situation is inevitable, and the best way to ensure its success will be in having a plan before it happens.

answer

Communication will be key to developing a plan with your husband. Discuss your individual and joint goals and plans regarding your careers, your choice of housing, and family concerns. Having a plan in place before a transfer or promotion is offered will mean that you and your husband already have the big-picture direction for your marriage and your family in mind.

Go through the various potential scenarios of job transfers and promotions, and make some decisions up front about what you will do. Virtual offices, telecommuting, and job sharing are just a few of the ways employers are making concessions that would allow one of you to continue your career in another location. One of you may have to give up something when a transfer or promotion is offered. Knowing that your marriage is more important than the job will make the decision clearer.

Change brings with it a degree of fear and uncertainty, which is usually the root cause of disagreement. Although change is inevitable when it comes to employment situations for you and your husband, conflict is not. Incorporating your plan and working together as a couple will draw you closer.

worth thinking about

▶ **When you already** know the direction of your marriage, most decisions you will be faced with have already been dealt with, regardless of the situation or circumstances.

▶ **It can be easy** to get carried away with the emotion of the situation. If that happens, take time to consider the offer individually, and talk about it calmly later.

▶ **If you don't** have a plan in place, write down the goals for your marriage and family you each have. Discuss any that are at odds. Resolve or adjust them now, before the conflict has a chance to grow.

This is what the LORD, who saves you, the Holy One of Israel, says: "I am the LORD your God, who teaches you to do what is good, who leads you in the way you should go."
Isaiah 48:17, NCV

12 question

How do you encourage him to accept a promotion?

It is exciting to see that your husband has been offered a promotion, and you think he should accept it. The employer offered him the job because he thought he could do it. Remember, it isn't what others think about his ability or the promotion itself. This is your husband's career and his final choice to make. He will want to know what effect this promotion will have on his career, his job satisfaction, and his family. You can help by knowing that he looks at the big picture, not at just the immediate promotion.

answer

Looking at the promotion through his eyes will enable you to be supportive of a good career choice. A promotion can have a big impact on your husband's career path. Some promotions will actually put him on the fast track to upper management, while others may land him in a dead-end position from which there is no going forward.

Ask your husband how you can help with the decision. Sometimes just being able to talk with you about it without feeling he has to have the decision already made will help him look at the various aspects of the promotion. When he is ready, sit down with him and discuss his abilities and aptitudes, as well as his current and potential work environment and his work relationships. Looking ahead to the next advancement will alert both of you to any career paths that would fail to move him forward. Also consider the length of time before current and potential supervisors and managers may retire, as this is a good indication of the next advancement opportunity.

While the opportunity for a promotion can be an exciting time for your husband and you, it is also a time to discuss his career plans in general and figure out how those plans fit into your marriage and your family. Your marriage and your family should always be more important than any job or promotion because you want to invest your energy in those things that last.

worth thinking about

▶ **If your husband** is a hands-on kind of guy, then a promotion to supervisor or manager may not be what he really wants. Consider if your desires for his promotion are for his best interests or for yours.

▶ **Be proud** of what your husband does, no matter what his position in the company is. Tell him often you appreciate that he goes to work and supports you and your family.

▶ **Whether your husband** accepts a promotion or not should not change how you feel about him or how you treat him. Love him as if he owned the company.

> *Think about the things of heaven,*
> *not the things of earth.*
> Colossians 3:2, NLT

13 — question

How do you balance work and recreation?

Men and women often fall into one of two extremes regarding the balance between work and play—either all work and no play, or all play and no work. Either of these situations can be frustrating. Understanding your husband's focus and knowing when it is appropriate to divert his attention from one extreme to the other will help both of you achieve your goals.

answer

It can be easy to think that working all the time will help you get ahead or, in some cases, even just catch up. You will find, however, that working all the time isn't the answer. Finding the right balance between work and play results in work being more productive and play being more refreshing.

Since your husband sees himself through the lens of his accomplishments, his career can be a measure of success for him. Encourage him to balance his success at work with his success in other areas of his life, including his marriage, his family, and his other relationships.

If you think there is an imbalance between your time spent at work and your time spent in play, talk to your husband about your concerns. Ask for his suggestions, and make some decisions together about your goals as a couple. Constant fatigue, irritation at little things, and feelings of being overwhelmed can be signs of too much time spent working.

There is nothing wrong with working hard, just as there is nothing wrong with taking time off. You can maintain a balance between the two by setting aside recreation time that is free of distractions and by ensuring that your time at work is productive.

worth thinking about

- ▶ **If you find** it difficult to get away for longer vacations because of work schedules, plan short getaways for two to three days at a time throughout the year.

- ▶ **The Bible says** that what you invest in is what you will have in the future. Keep your focus on what really reflects your values as a couple—your marriage, your family, and your faith.

- ▶ **If your expenses** are placing an additional burden on your husband, look for ways to scale back on spending without having to increase income.

You have six days each week for your ordinary work, but the seventh day is a Sabbath day of rest dedicated to the LORD your God.
Exodus 20:9–10, NLT

question

▼

Why does he need sex to feel loved?

One of the biggest mysteries in human physiology is the difference in sex drive between men and women. For your husband, the need for sex is as much physical as it is emotional. His need to connect physically with you is one expression of his desire to connect emotionally. Your husband sees your willingness to join physically with him as a demonstration of your love, vulnerability, and trust for him, because that is how he perceives his desire for you.

answer

▼

The male sex drive originates in the testicles and the gonads, which produce sperm and semen on an ongoing basis. These fluids are accumulated in the testicles, and they either need to be released through ejaculation or eventually get absorbed back into the body. This collection of seminal fluids drives the desire for sex, in much the same way as the accumulation of breast milk drives the need to nurse your baby. The sex act raises your husband's hormone levels, which causes feelings of satisfaction and fulfillment. The result is that he feels connected emotionally with you.

On the other hand, for women, the relationship is important. Your sex drive is based more in the emotional than the physical. This is why you probably find it difficult to be enthusiastic about sex after you and your husband have had a disagreement. For you, the emotional connection releases the sex hormones and fluids needed for stimulation and satisfaction.

Your husband views the sex act in a loving relationship as the highest compliment he could give to the woman he loves. His desire to connect with you demonstrates his degree of commitment to the marriage.

Understanding your husband's physiology will help you see that it isn't all about him or meeting his needs. He loves you, and he wants to show that love in one of the most intimate physical ways he knows how.

worth thinking about

▶ While love is important, sex is also integral to your marriage relationship. Choosing to meet your husband's physical needs is a demonstration of love that he can understand.

▶ Your husband's desire to meet with you emotionally shows his level of commitment to you and your marriage.

▶ True unity is the joining together of two separate entities. The physical and emotional union is an illustration of the unity that God put in place for marriage.

> *Husbands ought to love their wives as they love their own bodies. For a man who loves his wife actually shows love for himself.*
> Ephesians 5:28, NLT

15

question

What can you do if you don't feel sexy?

There are many circumstances that will steal your joy and enthusiasm for sex and intimacy, including lack of energy, unresolved conflict, outside distractions, and negative feelings of self-worth. Dealing with these barriers will open the doors to an enhanced sexual experience for both of you and will strengthen and deepen your marriage relationship. Feeling sexy and desirable will be a natural result of this stronger marriage, which will in turn cause more enthusiasm for your husband and your intimate times together.

answer

Lack of energy will not only sap your desire for sex but will also steal your physical, mental, and emotional health. Unresolved conflict between you and your husband will drive a wedge between you that will ultimately break down your relationship. Outside distractions such as television, recreation, and even jobs will place demands on you and your time, often pulling you in different directions. How you see yourself will impact how much enjoyment you receive from life in general, and from intimacy in particular.

The place to start is with how you feel about yourself. You were created by God to be a loving and sensitive creature, one capable of making good decisions. You are not a victim of your past, no matter how horrible that might be. When you understand how God feels about you, you will be able to see past your vision and into His. You are more than adequate to be wife, mother, friend, and whatever else your husband and your family need you to be.

worth thinking about

▶ **If you are always** tired, consider taking a vitamin or mineral supplement. American women tend to be deficient in magnesium and iron. Talk to your health-care adviser. Taking time to care for your physical needs gives you more energy for intimacy.

▶ **Your ability to give** and receive love and pleasure is directly related to whether you see yourself as worthy. Feeling worthy makes you more desirable.

▶ **Feeling sexy** is related to how you feel about yourself. Treat yourself to a manicure, take a long bubble bath, get a massage, or buy some pretty underwear. Your husband is worth the investment.

The marriage bed must be a place of mutuality— the husband seeking to satisfy his wife, the wife seeking to satisfy her husband.
1 Corinthians 7:3, THE MESSAGE

How do you let him know what really turns you on?

Let him kiss me with the kisses
of his mouth—for your love
is better than wine.

Song of Solomon 1:2, NKJV

16

question

Why do you feel that you're not woman enough for him?

Most feelings of inadequacy women experience are related to sexual intimacy, and that is usually because your husband wants to have sex more often than you do. While it is true that your husband will normally want to have sex more frequently than you do, quantity doesn't always equal quality. You will normally expend more emotional energy during sexual intercourse than he does, and sometimes you will need more time to replenish that energy as well. This in no way reflects on your abilities as a woman to please and satisfy your husband.

answer

Feelings of inadequacy can come from your own expectations, comments your husband makes, or comparisons of you to others, including people you know and models in advertisements. It is easy to fall prey to the lure of the seduction portrayed in media, and it is difficult to measure up to the media's standard of the perfect wife. Your husband can fall victim to the messages conveyed, and his comments may actually be a reflection of what he is seeing and hearing.

The best way to address your concerns is to discuss them with your husband. Ask him if there are areas of your intimate and public lives where he would like to see changes made. The changes should include things you can do as a couple.

Encourage your husband to initiate means other than intercourse to demonstrate his love for you. In turn, take a look at why you are not interested in sex more often, and make suggestions of how he might increase your interest.

It can be easy to read between the lines if he makes comments about not getting enough sex. Don't look for reasons to be insufficient—instead, look for reasons to celebrate your love, your marriage, and your commitment to each other.

worth thinking about

▶ **Encourage your husband** to begin the lovemaking process early in the day through loving words and special touches. Intimacy doesn't just begin once the bedroom door is closed.

▶ **Spend some extra time** on yourself today with a manicure, a pedicure, a facial, or even just a bubble bath. You are worth the extra time and energy, and you will feel better about yourself.

▶ **Buy some sexy nightwear,** and be prepared to not wear it very long. No matter what your body shape or age, lace and frills make every woman look desirable.

> *Be devoted to one another in brotherly love;*
> *give preference to one another in honor.*
> Romans 12:10, NAS

question

What do you do if he fails to satisfy you sexually?

While physical demonstration of love is important, it is not the only way to show love. Intimacy is not just about sex. Physical love is about knowing your husband personally and with commitment. Feeling dissatisfied sexually can stem from many reasons. Talk to your husband, and tell him your concerns. The keys to a successful sex life in your marriage are open and honest discussion and a willingness to make changes.

answer

Physiological differences between men and women result in differing levels of sexual satisfaction. Men have been described as being like a gas stove—quick to heat up and quick to cool down. Women, on the other hand, are like an electric stove—slow to heat up and slow to cool down.

Communicating this to your husband will go a long way toward allowing both of you to make changes in your sex pattern to accommodate your differing needs. Encourage foreplay to heighten and prolong the experience for both of you. Bear in mind that not every time you have intercourse will be the best you've ever had. Avoid rating each encounter, and instead approach each encounter with the expectation of pleasing your husband.

While sexual satisfaction contributes to your overall feeling of marital satisfaction, it should not be the only measurement you depend on. There are many reasons why you may be going through a less than satisfactory period of sex during your marriage. However, focusing on the good and the positive aspects of your marriage will encourage you to make changes where you can, and to persevere through those areas that may seem dry at the moment. You can find an oasis even in the deepest desert if you really look for it.

worth thinking about

▶ **Set the atmosphere** with candles or music. Take a shower together before you go to sleep, or use massage oils.

▶ **When you both** focus on pleasing each other, you take your attention off your pleasure, which can remove a lot of stress that is often associated with sex.

▶ **Consider what it** is about your sex life that is not satisfying you. Let him know what you like and what you don't like. Ask him what he'd like you to do differently. Consider changing positions, locations, or even the time of day or day of the week you normally have sex.

> *Marriage is not a place to "stand up for your rights." Marriage is a decision to serve the other, whether in bed or out.*
> 1 Corinthians 7:4, THE MESSAGE

question

What aphrodisiacs work?

In this busy world, it is sometimes easy to fall into a pattern or a rut with the intimate side of your marriage. Maybe you've even thought that your sex life could use a little spicing up. Images of oysters and strawberries and rhinoceros horn are probably dancing through your mind at the term *aphrodisiac*. The fact is, many times the best aphrodisiac is the attitude you have toward your husband and your intimate times together.

answer

Regardless of the length of time married, most couples would agree that an exciting sex life is one of the major perks and is often the first thing to fall by the wayside. Lack of attention given to each other because of the demands of jobs, children, and other distractions can diminish time and energy left over at the end of the day.

The good news is that with very little effort, you can bring the excitement back into your marital relations without spending a fortune on remedies that may or may not produce the desired effects. In fact, studies have shown that how spouses feel about each other has more impact on sexual arousal than aphrodisiacs.

Knowing how your husband understands love will help you show him that you desire him long before you ever get to the bedroom. Everything you say and do impacts his perception of his worth to you.

You and your husband are sensual beings, so use all of your senses in creating a cocoon of intimacy between you. You both should feel safe with each other, and able to freely express what pleases you and what doesn't. Don't feel that you'll hurt each other if you tell each other what you really like. You want to please him, and he wants to please you. That's what it's all about! Agree beforehand that this time together is a joy-filled journey, and resolve to end the journey in a loving and wonderful place.

worth thinking about

▶ Treating yourselves to a new set of sheets for your bed can create a romantic aura for you, so choose satin, silk, or a high-quality percale that feels good on your bare skin.

▶ Touching is important to sexual arousal, so spend an extended period of time exploring each other's bodies. Use oils or scented creams to massage each other.

▶ Speaking words of love and respect to your husband can be more of a turn-on for him than any amount of oysters or strawberries!

> *My lover wouldn't take no for an answer, and the longer he knocked, the more excited I became.*
> Song of Solomon 5:4, THE MESSAGE

▼

How can you show him it isn't all about sex?

Your marriage isn't all about sex. Your love for your husband doesn't rely entirely on your demonstrating it with sex. The faithfulness, commitment, and affection you show outside the bedroom are the examples you set for your children. Sometimes it seems as if men know how to show their love and commitment only through sex, and that can be frustrating. You can demonstrate to your husband that while sex is important to you, it isn't the only way you show love.

answer

▼

You can begin by making sure you have time together every day to talk without distraction about the things that happened that day that were important to you. Set this time aside, schedule it into your calendar if need be, and don't allow anything to interfere. Focus entirely on your husband, and listen to what he is telling you. These will be the issues that are impacting how he thinks and acts.

Remind your husband that sex isn't always the goal by making sure that not all intimate times end in sex. Cuddling is good, just lying close to your husband and allowing your hands to explore and massage in a nonsexual way. Kisses, touches, whispered words, and glances can communicate your love for each other. Put on some favorite music, and dance close together for no reason other than that you want to.

Sex without love and intimacy is empty and not fulfilling. Love and intimacy don't begin and end with sex. You can encourage your husband to show his love and his feelings for you in ways other than sex, but you should also be willing to allow him to show you how much he loves you through sex. Marital love and intimacy should be fulfilling and satisfying for both of you. The secret is to find a balance between sex and intimacy such that your needs and your husband's needs are being met.

worth thinking about

▶ Talk to your husband about his perception of your love for him. Strengthen any areas that he might have doubts about.

▶ While many marriages in which there are health issues thrive without sex, lack of sex can put a stress on your marriage. If sex is physically difficult, find other ways to show your love and create intimacy between you and your husband.

▶ There are several well-written and well-illustrated resource books available that tastefully and conservatively describe alternate sexual positions and techniques. Read these books together as a couple.

> *Do not deprive each other except by mutual consent and for a time, so that you may devote yourselves to prayer. Then come together again.*
> 1 Corinthians 7:5, NIV

question

▼

How do you help him overcome his attraction to pornography?

Men get caught in the web of pornography for many reasons. Pornography touches the area of their brains that is highly sensitive to visual imagery. And pornography retains its hold because a man's sex drive is visually stimulated much more than a woman's. You can help him break this cycle by letting him know he is not alone in this prison in his mind and that you love him and want him to share his sexual desires with you in a much more fulfilling way than pornography can ever provide.

answer

▼

Men are told pornography will make them better lovers and that it demonstrates that women are beautiful and need to be glorified. In a 2005 Summit on Pornography, Daniel Weiss from Focus on the Family revealed that men who are addicted to pornography tend to have lower opinions of women, relegating them to sex objects for their own pleasure.

The visual stimulation of pornography releases endorphins and other chemicals into the brain. This creates a desire for more and more, and eventually this desire becomes a physiological need, much the same as an addiction to alcohol or any other drug.

Talking to your husband about your concerns with pornography and the effect it has on your marriage will bring it out into the open and will stop the secret shame your husband has likely been experiencing over his struggles with pornography.

The very nature of pornography—the guilt/pleasure cycle—causes men to avoid seeking help. Often what happens is that your husband will tend to feel less of himself as a man the longer he is caught in the web of lies that pornography weaves. The good news is pornography is one of those secret areas of a man's life that once exposed cannot retain its hold over him.

worth thinking about

▶ There are many support groups available for men and couples who want to overcome the problems caused by pornography in their homes and their marriages.

▶ Pornography is not limited to adults—children are being exposed at younger ages, at a time when their own sexuality and their perception of sexuality are being defined.

▶ Pornography is not harmless adult entertainment; you and your husband need to take a stand for the sanctity of marriage and sexual intimacy.

> *Only those whose hands and hearts are pure, who do not worship idols and never tell lies . . . will receive the Lord's blessing and have right standing with God their savior.*
> Psalm 24:4–5, NLT

question

How do you
show him you
are not his mother?

It can be easy to fall into a pattern of doing so much for your husband that you make him dependent on you. Over time, an attitude of servanthood can cause your relationship to change from that of a husband and his wife to that of a boy and his mother. You can best show him you are not his mother first by not perpetuating an attitude of dependency, and second by maintaining an atmosphere of intimacy between you.

answer

Your husband's mother played an important role in his life, nurturing him and teaching him how to become an independent person in his own right. Even though you may do some of the same things his mother did, you do them for a different reason. You do them because you and your husband are a team, each with a part to play.

You can perpetuate an attitude of independence by encouraging him to participate in the operations of your household through the sharing of chores and responsibilities. Discuss together your expectations regarding participation, and assign responsibility accordingly. You may find your husband wasn't trying to avoid helping out but was instead simply unaware of your concerns.

You can maintain an atmosphere of intimacy through daily affirmation, special touches and looks passed between you during the day, and the physical expression of your love through your sex life. Don't allow the distractions of the day to detract from the physical side of your marriage.

Your husband didn't marry you because he needed someone to look after him or to cook and clean for him. You don't need to act like his servant. Treat him as your best friend, your lover, and your hero, and he will be quick to respond by treating you like the diva you are.

worth thinking about

▶ **If finances permit**, hire someone to do some of the chores neither of you enjoys doing.

▶ **Always telling him** what to do is one symptom of acting like a mother. If you see this in your behavior, change your telling to asking. Allow him ownership of a solution.

▶ **Independence doesn't** mean your husband can handle everything on his own. Independence is about his ability to make informed decisions, to carry out those decisions, and to take responsibility for his actions.

> *I am my lover's and my lover is mine.*
> Song of Solomon 6:3, NIV

question

▾

Why is he jealous of the time you spend with the kids?

The fact that your husband wants to spend more time with you is a good thing. However, his perception that the kids are interfering with that time together may be an insecurity he is feeling. His actual feelings may not be related to the amount of time you spend with the children but instead may spring from the feeling that you don't have any energy left over for him. Another reason he may be jealous is that you really are spending an inordinate amount of time with the children.

answer

▾

Your husband works hard to maintain your household, and that work is important to him. His primary goals in your marriage are to ensure the safety and comfort of his family, and your focus will be on the relationships within your family. For you, spending time with your children is one of the ways you develop deeper relationships with them.

One thing to remember is that you will also develop a deeper and more intimate relationship with your husband as you spend time with him. Since your relationship with your husband should be even more important than your relationship with your children, it is important to schedule your time together as a couple.

Make sure you allow time each day for you to sit down with your husband, go over the events of the day, and unwind with each other.

Don't ignore your husband's feelings of resentment about the time you spend with your children. Address the problem immediately and allow him to express his concerns, even if you think they are unimportant or even childish. Encourage your husband to share in the time you spend with the children so that it becomes family time.

worth thinking about

▶ **Your husband doesn't** want you to ignore your children; he just wants you to allocate some of your time to him. Make that time special by lighting a few candles or turning on some soft background music.

▶ **Date times** are important to maintaining your connectedness as a couple. Plan something special for your next date night.

▶ **Including your husband** in the time you spend with the kids will allow him to see the progress they are making in their schoolwork, and also give him a sense of ownership in their accomplishments.

> *With each of you we were like a father with his child, holding your hand, whispering encouragement, showing you step-by-step how to live well before God.*
>
> 1 Thessalonians 2:11–12, THE MESSAGE

23

question
▼

How do you teach your children to encourage their father?

Your children love their father, and a natural outflow of that love is their desire to encourage and edify. They may have trouble, however, putting their feelings into actions and words. Children will tend to imitate what they see in their everyday lives. You can teach your children to encourage their father by setting the example for them as well as by making age-appropriate suggestions.

answer
▼

Share with your children some of the ways you show your encouragement and support for their father. When children see consistency in your actions and attitudes, they are more likely to adopt them as their own. One way is to openly show your love for your husband with appropriate public displays of affection and to encourage your children to show their love in appropriate ways as well.

Knowing how your husband understands and receives love—his love language—will also help you teach your children how to show their love for and support of their father in ways he will see and understand. Encouraging your children to participate in family decisions and planning will allow them to see not only their place within the family, but also their value as members of a cohesive unit.

Teach your children to give encouragement to their father in tangible ways, including spending time with him. To a father, having a child want to be with him is one of the highest honors he can receive.

Too often today, a mother and a father raising their children together is a rarity. More than 25 percent of the children in America are being raised in single-parent households. Your children probably have at least one friend who is in this situation. When your children appreciate the stability of your family and your marriage, it will be easier for them to see the good in their father and to thank him and support him for his role in their lives.

worth thinking about

▶ Your children want a father they can look up to and admire. In recent studies, more than 50 percent of children said their father was their idea of a superhero.

▶ Actions can speak louder than words. Help your children show their appreciation through cards, crafts, and voluntary chores.

▶ Sometimes just wanting to spend time together can be encouraging to your husband. Try to arrange at least ten minutes per day for each child to spend one-on-one with their dad.

> *He's going to see his children, my personal gift to him—lots of children. And these children will honor me by living holy lives.*
> Isaiah 29:23, THE MESSAGE

24

Why is his relationship with the children important?

There are many reasons why people choose to have children, including the creation of a beautiful new life as a symbol of the love between husband and wife, for the unconditional love given and received, and to ensure the family name will be carried on by descendants. Regardless of the reason for having children, most people would say that the reason is secondary to the relationship that develops between parent and child.

answer

Your husband determines his success as a father based on his perception of his relationship with his children, which will take many forms as the children grow up. At first he may be involved on a more peripheral level by providing you with the time and resources to care for and nurture the infant. As more children come along, he may take a more involved role in caring for the older children, once again freeing you to fill the role of nurturing caretaker for the infants.

As your children develop communication skills, your husband's role will expand to teaching social rules and manners, as well as developing physical skills. As your husband takes on this role as teacher, your children learn trust and respect as well as valuable life lessons in work and play activities.

Through the school years it is important that your husband's relationship with his children include helping them with their schoolwork and projects, which demonstrates to your children that he is an intelligent man with many abilities they may not see in the normal course of the day.

Regardless of your children's ages, it is never too late to deepen their relationship with their father. He is an integral part of their lives, important to their social development and to their understanding of how men and women communicate and treat each other. Your marriage is the training ground for theirs, and your good example will go a long way toward ensuring the success of their future marriages.

worth thinking about

▶ **Your husband's** role in your older child's development is an important part of the maturing process as your husband demonstrates that each person contributes to the running of the household and caring for one another.

▶ **Fathers are important**—daughters tend to choose men that are like their father, and sons tend to treat their wives following the example their fathers gave.

▶ **You can encourage** a deeper relationship between your husband and children by arranging for each child to have one day on a regular basis to spend with their dad.

The father of a good child is very happy; parents who have wise children are glad because of them.
Proverbs 23:24, NCV

question

How do you encourage him to spend time with the kids?

It can be easy to get so caught up in the process of earning a living that your husband forgets the purpose of his job—to support his family and to provide for their needs. You can encourage your husband to spend time with his children by reminding him that they need him more than they need the things you can buy with his income, and that the example he sets for them by working faithfully is not as important as their knowing how much they mean to him.

answer

When a man spends a lot of time away from his children, he may begin to feel disconnected from them and believe he doesn't have anything in common with them. The truth of the matter is that he is their father, he loves their mother, and he chooses to be true and faithful to her. That is the biggest common bond they have.

In addition to that, children look up to their fathers as role models and mentors. Children desperately want to believe that someone has their best interests at heart and that no matter what else happens around them, they will always have a safe relationship they can depend on—their family.

When you treat your husband with respect and teach your children to respect him, he sees that he has an important place in your family. Focusing on his abilities other than his job and bringing home a paycheck is important to his self-validation. Including him in family activities and even arranging activities around his work schedule tells him he is important to you.

Choosing to spend time with him as a family shows him you would rather be where he is than anywhere else. When your husband feels valued and needed, he will be more likely to invest his time with you and your children.

worth thinking about

▶ Change your focus from the things you buy with your husband's paycheck to activities that the whole family can do together.

▶ Plan a special family time where no money is involved, and include the kids in the planning. Let them know you are not spending money specifically because you want to show them money is not the most important thing—family is.

▶ Do some research into youth activities available in your community that your kids are interested in, and ask about the need for adult volunteers. Talk to your husband, and both of you sign up to participate with your kids.

> *In everything set them an example by doing what is good. In your teaching show integrity.*
> Titus 2:7, NIV

How do you help him dream a bigger dream?

I will pour out my Spirit on all people. Your sons and daughters will prophesy, your old men will dream dreams, your young men will see visions.

Joel 2:28, NIV

26

Why does he have such high expectations of your children?

Many years ago, husbands went to work and brought home their paychecks. Wives stayed home, raised the children, and took care of the house. However, society today demands much more from men regarding their ability to support their families, their participation in their families, and their relationships with their wives. Men realize that in order to succeed in all these areas of their lives, they must be more prepared to take on the challenge.

answer

Your husband's expectations of his children stem from the pressures being placed on him as husband and father. Regardless of how well equipped he may be for the task, undoubtedly there are areas where he feels less than adequate in what is expected of him. As a good father, he doesn't want to see his children struggling in these areas when they become adults.

As fathers become more involved in child rearing, they often see areas where they feel their own fathers fell short in their training. This can be especially true if your husband came from a single-parent household. If this is the case, your husband may overcompensate with your children to ensure this perceived shortfall doesn't affect them.

Your child has a unique combination of talents and interests, and your job as parents is to encourage him to develop into a productive member of society and fulfill his dreams and goals, not yours. As your husband spends time with your children, he will begin to see how well they are developing, not only academically but also with regard to their character and friendships. Make time to talk over any concerns he might have, and be able to set his mind at ease that he is raising really good kids.

worth thinking about

▶ **High expectations** never hurt anyone; what may hurt is the feeling associated with failing to meet those expectations. Talk to your children and address any concerns they may have.

▶ **If you are concerned** about your husband's expectations, talk to him. Share your expectations, and then decide which ones he might relax and which ones you might increase.

▶ **High expectations** are relative. Consider the purpose of the expectation as well as the child involved. What is right for one child may be unattainable for another.

> *Blessed is the man who endures temptation; for when he has been approved, he will receive the crown of life which the Lord has promised to those who love Him.*
>
> James 1:12, NKJV

question

▼

How do you get him to not play so rough with your kids?

Physical play often involves unintentional minor injury. When your children play with other children, it is likely that someone skins a knee or knocks a head. It can be easy watching from the sidelines to think that your husband is playing too rough with your children. Your goal is to determine if he really is playing too rough or if they are putting on an act for you, and then to talk with your husband about any concerns you might have.

answer

▼

If your kids see that you will give them rewards and preferential treatment every time they complain of an ache or a bruise, you can expect they will milk that for all it is worth, particularly if your response is greater when that small injury comes from playing with their father. Your best response is to make sure the injury is minor, clean any scrape, and then send your child back to play.

If you think your husband's play is resulting in more than an ordinary number of bruises or other small injuries, talk to him about your concerns when the children are not present. Have specific examples in mind, and discuss the situation calmly and rationally. There is a very good chance that your husband may not realize you are concerned.

To raise responsible children, you need to encourage fair play, consistent rules, and respect for others. When your husband and children are playing together, their relationship is deepened, and your children will be challenged physically and intellectually. You know your husband wants to raise good kids. Trust him to do what is best for them.

worth thinking about

▶ **There is a fine line** between rough play and bullying. Listen to your children to sense how they feel about the way their father plays with them. If they don't voice any concerns, then relax and let them enjoy their time with their dad.

▶ **You may be** able to make their play gentler if you participate. If they are playing a game you don't know the rules for, ask them to teach you. Most children are delighted to be able to teach their parents something.

▶ **If you are still concerned**, as a couple ask a trusted friend or adviser to watch your husband and children play together.

Pursue righteousness, godliness, faith, love, endurance and gentleness.
1 Timothy 6:11, NIV

question

▼

What if you don't agree with his child-discipline methods?

Marriage is about taking two different people and bring-ing them together, creating a relationship in which the individual ideas and abilities of each spouse enhance and complement the other. You and your husband prob-ably didn't agree on everything when you got married, and you have likely made some changes and perhaps even some compromises on issues such as finances, cooking, and careers. Even if you agreed on everything else, the disciplining of your children may still cause some contention. You and your husband need to decide who will be the primary disciplinarian and set some guidelines for the use of discipline.

answer

▼

Once children know which parent will mete out disci-pline, they will be sure to run to the other parent in an attempt to work one against the other. An important point to remember is that regardless of which parent has delivered the discipline, the other parent should not speak out against that in front of the child.

For discipline to be effective, unity is imperative. If your children learn to manipulate one of you against the other, your attempts at discipline are thwarted. Showing unity in your decision will be the best way to limit any refereeing by the other parent and will let your children know who has the final say regarding discipline.

Discussions regarding discipline are best done in private when the children are not present. Decide before the children are even born what your preferred methods of discipline are, and have a plan in place to deal with the common issues that will come up. If you are now caught in a cycle of disagreement regarding form and extent of discipline, sit down and talk it over with your husband.

worth thinking about

▶ Make sure discipline is always the result of wanting what is best for your child.

▶ Discipline is not just punishment. Discipline is about changing behavior to conform to standards or expectations. Make sure you are not expecting your children to obey rules you are not following.

▶ Talk to your children about what you expect of them; you might be surprised to find that your children really do want to know what their boundaries are.

> *[Our earthly fathers] disciplined us for a short time as seemed best to them, but He disciplines us for our good, so that we may share His holiness.*
>
> Hebrews 12:10, NAS

What makes a husband successful?

Popular opinion would have you believe you can guarantee your husband's success by doing specific things. While that may sound appealing, your husband would prefer you understand that your concept of success and his might be different because you look at criteria such as job status, finances, and family structure differently. You can choose to support him by knowing how he defines success, and then by helping him succeed in those areas.

answer

Your husband's definition of success is going to depend on where his priorities lie. He will know if he has been successful in achieving his priorities by comparing where he was and is with where he wants to be. One way he measures that is through goals. Your husband feels goals and plans must be measurable and tangible. Success for him will be the accomplishment or achievement of specific goals.

You can be part of your husband's success by asking how you might help him achieve his goals and dreams. Sometimes those goals and dreams will be nonspecific; encourage him to quantify those goals and to put a value and a time frame on them so that he can determine how close he is to achieving them.

There are many good resources available to help you both develop your goals into strategies. One of the best sources is the Bible, a how-to book on marriage, parenthood, relationships, and good business practices.

Sharing your goals and dreams with your husband, and asking him to share his with you, will create more unity and togetherness in your marriage. Seeing that you are working together toward the same outcome will encourage you to stick to the plan and will allow both of you to be part of your individual successes, as well as the overall success of your marriage.

worth thinking about

- ▶ If your husband's goals are vague, such as he wants to have a "good" marriage, ask him to define how he wants to accomplish that and what his benchmarks of success would be.

- ▶ Studies have shown that more than 80 percent of people who write down their goals will achieve them. By the same token, more than 80 percent of people who do not write down their goals will not achieve them. Be achievers—write your goals down.

- ▶ Include your children where applicable in your plans and dreams. Encourage them to develop goals and plans of their own.

> The LORD your God will prosper you abundantly in all the work of your hand.
>
> Deuteronomy 30:9, NAS

30

question

▼

How do you avoid pestering him?

Pestering or nagging is usually the result of perceived inactivity. You think he should be doing something, and he isn't. Quite often what happens when you do pester him is that he resists your efforts to direct his actions. Getting your focus off what you want him to do and on what he needs to do to accomplish the goals of your marriage is key to not getting into the cycle of pestering and resisting.

answer

▼

You can start with sitting down and talking with your husband about the frustrations you are experiencing. Each of you can compile your own to-do list of short-term and long-term projects and goals. If possible, include how much time and money will be needed to do the job. Compare personal lists, prioritize them, and determine which projects are not necessary or can be delayed. Decide who will complete the tasks based on abilities and timing.

Commit a time to begin the project at hand and decide to sit down again in a few weeks and see how you are progressing. This gives you the opportunity to revise the lists as needed, as well as to acknowledge your accomplishments.

Pestering or nagging isn't only about to-do lists. Everyday activities, such as taking out the trash or putting dishes in the dishwasher, can also become points of contention. Talk to your husband about any issue that irritates you, and consider his input. There will probably be areas where compromise will be needed, but in most cases you will find that calm discussion will accomplish more than nagging.

You are both on the same team and want what is best for your marriage and your family. Reminding each other of that, and making sure you are spending quality time together and not just making busywork, will go a long way in strengthening your marriage.

worth thinking about

▶ **Concentrating on** your individual to-do lists will take your focus off your perception of what the other person isn't doing and put it on what is getting done.

▶ **Try to include** several projects that you can work on together. The time you spend accomplishing a task is important to your sense of unity, creating a feeling of teamwork and celebrating shared victories.

▶ **Include your kids** or family in the process of accomplishing a project that benefits the whole family.

> *A foolish son is destruction to his father, and the contentions of a wife are a constant dripping.*
> Proverbs 19:13, NAS

question

Why does he need your encouragement?

Your husband married you for more than just to have a wife and a mother of his children. He married you because he needs you—that is the way God created him. His rational, logical, solution-oriented side needs your relationship-building and caring side to be complete. Part of the way you were created makes you want to nurture, and while your husband doesn't need you to mother him, he does need your praise, support, and encouragement to confirm he is on the right track.

answer

Fulfillment of your husband's need for work gives him a sense of accomplishment and significance. However, needing to feel good about himself can also enslave him as he strives to retain that feeling of significance. In most cases, other people in your husband's life won't be as attuned to his emotional needs as you are, and this is where your encouragement becomes critical.

Being an encourager of your husband doesn't mean you make him dependent on you for his sense of self-worth. On the contrary, his sense of self-worth is actually strengthened by your support. In much the same way as nails hold a board in place, your encouragement is a stabilizer for your husband. The strength is in the board; the stability is in the nails and their placement.

Your encouragement tells your husband that you believe in what he is doing. When you give him sincere praise, he will understand your love for him in a concrete way. In choosing to encourage him, it is important to be willing to withhold your advice until he asks for it, and to allow him to bounce ideas off you before he makes an important decision.

When your husband looks good, you look good. When your husband feels good about himself, he will feel good about you and your marriage. Look for ways to encourage him every day, and very soon you will feel that encouragement flowing back to you.

worth thinking about

▶ **If your husband** takes a briefcase or lunch to work, tuck a short note inside that tells him you appreciate something he recently said or did.

▶ **Tell your husband** often that you appreciate him and his hard work for your family.

▶ **The Bible has many** examples of people who overcame difficult situations. Suggest you read together an account of David, Daniel, Joshua, or Nehemiah for encouragement.

> *My life is an example to many, because you have been my strength and protection.*
> Psalm 71:7, NLT

question

▼

How do you support him when he struggles with a decision?

Wrestling with a decision is not a sign of weakness or inability on your husband's part. If he struggles, it is because he wants to make the best decision possible. Reminding him that you are there to help if he needs you and that you know he can make a good decision may be all he needs to go forward and take some action. Suggesting other resources may encourage him that he isn't alone in the decision-making process.

answer

▼

Often your husband will struggle with a decision because he feels he doesn't have enough information to make the right choice. Because of this, the part you play in helping him make the decision is very important. Remember that decision making requires information. Be prepared to supply him with whatever information and help he needs to gather the details required to solve the problem. Offer your help to do some research, perhaps through phone calls, or even on the Internet or at the library.

You can know if your husband is struggling by the way he reacts when you talk about a problem with him. He may want to talk about the decision all the time, putting forward numerous solutions but never choosing one.

Alternatively, he may refuse to discuss it at all. Help him free his energies for the decision-making process by encouraging him that you know he can choose the best course of action available given the circumstances.

When you see a delay in the decision being made, ask if there is something you can do to help.

If you see he is really getting bogged down in making a decision, suggest he talk to someone else about it. Remind him of someone he knows who has made a similar decision in the past. Remind your husband that others have gone through the same thing, and that those people could be a good source of information.

worth thinking about

▶ **Remind your husband** of past victories on similar decisions. In the Bible, recalling past victories against the lion and the bear strengthened David's resolve when he faced Goliath.

▶ **If he declines** your offer of help, let him know you are available should he think of something in the future. Keep the doors of communication open.

▶ **Sometimes the best** solution for a dilemma is to sleep on it. Suggest to your husband that he wait until the next day, when the solution may be more obvious.

> *Let the wise listen to these proverbs and become even wiser. Let those with understanding receive guidance.*
> Proverbs 1:5, NLT

question
▼
How do you help him persevere when things go wrong?

It can be discouraging and disheartening to not have things work out the way you expected them to. Whether because of a poor choice or as a result of outside circumstances that you had no control over, things will go wrong from time to time. How you view these situations, as catastrophe or as opportunity to overcome, will determine the outcome for you as individuals and as a couple.

answer
▼

Failure or even perceived failure can often be harder on your husband than it is on you. Men are very much success-driven, and their accomplishments reflect on them and their abilities in a personal way. Reminding your husband of his past achievements will help take his mind off his perception of failing.

Rather than wallowing in the situation, action is often the best way to overcome. Together look for a solution to the problem, even if it appears to be out of your control. An attitude of victory will make both of you feel like winners.

It is important not to place blame on each other or make accusations, no matter what the reason for the bad outcome. Determine that you are in this together and that together you will get through it. Agreement on a solution is important, because together you are stronger than you are individually.

Sometimes the best course of action when all around you seems to be falling apart is to take some of the rubble and start rebuilding. Talk to someone who has gone through a similar situation and apply what he learned. Pick up the pieces and get on with the rebuilding. Few situations are so bleak that there is absolutely no good to be found. Look for the silver lining in the storm cloud, and grab on to the hope you find there.

worth thinking about

▶ **If your husband** doesn't respond to your attempts to move his mind from failure to the solution, it is especially important that you keep a good attitude.

▶ **Encourage him,** praise him even in small things, and choose to move on with your lives. Make plans for the near and distant future.

▶ **Address and voice** any fears you may have individually and as a couple. Determine a course of action to deal with those fears.

▼

Be joyful in hope, patient in affliction, faithful in prayer.
Romans 12:12, NIV

question

How does your example help him be an encourager?

Few people start out in life not wanting to be positive or encouraging. Many people end up that way primarily because they don't have good role models. Just as setting a good example for your children is an important factor in their learning to act and speak in uplifting and edifying ways, sometimes it is necessary for your husband to be able to look to you as the example he wants to follow.

answer

You can indirectly help your husband become an encourager through your words and actions of edification. Being an encourager doesn't mean always having a smile or never having a bad-attitude moment. True encouragers are those who look past the momentary situation and at the larger picture. An encourager reflects the good attitudes of others, while deflecting the bad attitudes.

Keep in mind that as your husband begins to look to you as a role model for positive attitudes, you will probably have situations where you will be challenged to set a good example. Your husband doesn't want to see that your good outlook ensures nothing ever goes wrong for you; he will be much more interested in seeing how you handle a crisis or a problem.

Practice patience, serenity, and a calm confidence in all situations, whether inconsequential or more significant. This will become a habit that ingrains itself in your sate of mind.

Being positive is not difficult, and he will feel better about you and himself as he learns to become an encourager. As you look for ways to encourage him, he will respond by looking for ways to edify you and others around him. Your attitude will not only set the example, it will also be an encouragement for him.

worth thinking about

▶ **You can turn almost** any situation into a teaching moment. Be careful of your attitude when your husband is around, especially if he tends to be quick to look at the negative.

▶ **If you notice** your husband has been encouraging in his attitude and actions, be sure to compliment him.

▶ **Changing behavior** doesn't happen overnight. Be patient with your husband and with yourself as you both learn how to be encouragers.

> *Be an example to the believers with your words, your actions, your love, your faith, and your pure life.*
> 1 Timothy 4:12, NCV

question

How do you encourage him with your common interests?

One of your desires is to spend time with your husband, getting to know him better, and having him know you better. Your husband will probably not be satisfied sitting and talking unless he feels something else is being accomplished. One of the best ways to accomplish your goal of time together and his goal of doing is to find something to do together that accomplishes both of your goals. This can be a hobby, a fix-it project, or even just a walk around the block.

answer

You might choose to volunteer together on a community project, where your time spent benefits more than just you. You will not only see a tangible result of your efforts, but you will also feel a sense of belonging and ownership in the project.

Working on a project together around the house is another way to spend time without just sitting and talking. Again, this accomplishes your husband's desire to solve a problem and your desire to spend time together. It is best if these projects are done for the overall improvement of your home and not just to create busywork, which your husband will soon see as unproductive.

Doing something together doesn't always have to provide a tangible outcome. Taking a walk is a good form of exercise, which your husband would view as a positive reason to walk. You see walking as a way to talk over the day without distractions. Both of you feel you have accomplished something.

Common interests need to be just that—things both of you like doing well enough to want to do them together. Show enthusiasm for projects he suggests, even if you aren't sure you will like the activities. Spending time together is the primary focus.

worth thinking about

▶ **Individually make** a list of what you like to do. Compare lists, and see what you have in common. You may not even realize you both like to do similar activities.

▶ **If purpose** is important to you, consider some longer-term projects you might like to take part in. There are many organizations that provide room and board for a week or more on their property while you do repairs for them.

▶ **If you struggle** to find something in common that you like, find something completely new. Take dance lessons, join an amateur theater, or volunteer at the local animal shelter.

> *I say to you, that if two of you agree on earth about anything that they may ask, it shall be done for them by My Father who is in heaven.*
> Matthew 18:19, NAS

question

How can you help him feel confident in your marriage?

answer

Though an army may encamp against me, my heart shall not fear; though war may rise against me, in this I will be confident.

Psalm 27:3, NKJV

36

How do you help your husband admit when he is wrong?

It is never pleasant to admit when you've made a mistake, and if you are uncomfortable, your husband is even more so. Regardless of why he doesn't like to admit he is wrong, you can help him see that admitting wrong is not a sign of failure and in no way undermines his ability to lead your family; in fact, being quick to admit he is wrong shows strength of character and leadership.

answer

True leaders recognize quickly if they make a mistake and respond instantly with a course of action to correct that mistake. A sign of leadership is to admit to an error before anyone has the chance to accuse you of making it. Apologizing for a mistake will quickly diffuse anger and open the doors to a solution.

You can help your husband by admitting when you make a mistake. Do it publicly if you made the mistake publicly. Include all parties who know about your mistake. In this way, you show your husband that admitting an error tends to cause people to think better of you, not worse, and shows him that you make mistakes and you know you make them.

When admitting a mistake, be sure not to cast blame on anyone else or to rationalize your action or decision. To do so would act to mitigte your responsibility and to shrink personal accountability.

When your husband sees that making a bad decision or a mistake doesn't change the way you feel about him, he will not be so hesitant to admit wrong. Your support of him during this time is critical, so look for ways to encourage him in his decision-making processes so that he makes better choices that benefit both of you.

worth thinking about

- ▶ **You can help** your husband admit a wrong by taking ownership of a bad decision as a couple. When you admit that together you made a bad choice, you don't lay all the blame on any one person.

- ▶ **Talk to your husband** about your concerns, and ask how you can help. Suggest you pray together as a couple for guidance and wisdom for both of you.

- ▶ **If the mistake** is a recurring one that hurts your feelings such as forgetting your anniversary or birthday, offer to set up a reminder for him such as an online calendar system, or note the occasions in his calendar several days in advance so he has time to plan something special.

> *You are forgiving and good, O Lord,*
> *abounding in love to all who call to you.*
> Psalm 86:5, NIV

question

▼

How can you help him accomplish his goals while meeting your needs?

While marriage is like a joint venture between two people that is designed to enable them to accomplish goals they would likely not be able to reach individually, you and your husband are still separate people, each with your own personal goals and needs. In the best marriages, the individual goals augment the joint goals, and the couple finds a way to satisfy both the joint and individual goals. However, sometimes the individual can get overlooked in a marriage, and it is to the benefit of your husband and your marriage if you can make sure that both of you are feeling fulfilled in your relationship.

answer

▼

It can be easy to get caught up in working toward your goals as a couple, as spouses, and as parents. Many times your personal and individual needs may get overlooked, or there may simply not be enough time, energy, or other resources left over to accomplish them. The first thing you and your husband can do is to discuss what your individual needs may be. You can give him some concrete examples of how you would like to satisfy your needs, and you can ask him for some suggestions for satisfying his own needs. You may also consider how you may work together to accomplish more and also free up more time for both of you.

Next, you both can acknowledge that if you don't set aside the time, energy, and resources needed to meet your individual needs, it isn't likely to happen on its own. Realistically look at your schedules and available resources, and decide if there are any activities you might be able to drop or delegate to someone else.

While at first you may feel that focusing on your husband's goals will deter you from meeting your own needs, when your husband feels fulfilled physically, emotionally, and spiritually, he will in turn have more time and energy to help you meet your needs.

worth thinking about

▶ **If you don't already** have one, start a family calendar, a central location where you can schedule in your activities and commitments.

▶ **Include everyone** in the family in the planning. It may be that one of the activities you need to discontinue will be something another family member is involved in.

▶ **If your husband** offers to take on a task to give you some free time, thank him and encourage him even if he doesn't do it exactly the way you would have done it.

> *Do not be anxious about anything, but in everything, by prayer and petition, with thanksgiving, present your requests to God.*
> Philippians 4:6, NIV

question

How do you avoid comparing him with other women's husbands?

If you find yourself comparing your husband to other men, and particularly to other women's husbands, it can be an indication of dissatisfaction on your part. For whatever reason, you think you see something in the other man that your husband lacks. Marriage is meant to draw two people closer in unity, and comparison tends to divide. Rather than look for reasons to compare, you need to seek reasons to unite you and your husband in your marriage relationship.

answer

It is difficult to compare two things without tearing down one or the other. Comparison usually highlights and magnifies faults in one, ignoring the strengths. This can happen too easily if you compare your husband to another man. You intimately know your husband's strengths and faults, especially his faults, while you don't necessarily know the other man's faults to the same degree. This puts your husband at an unfair disadvantage.

Instead of looking at faults, concentrate on your husband's good points. Remind yourself of his strengths, be encouraged by those areas where he excels, and recall his past successes. How you think about your husband will direct how you feel about him.

Comparing may bring some sense of satisfaction or validation of your thoughts. However, true satisfaction comes only through a change of attitude. For your marriage to succeed, you need to embrace the attitude that you chose your husband as the man you wanted to be married to for the rest of your life. He is not perfect, but neither are you. Together you can work out the wrinkles and be better spouses to each other and for each other.

worth thinking about

▶ **Never discuss** your husband negatively with a male friend under the guise of seeking advice. Instead, discuss your concerns about your behavior with a trusted female friend who supports your marriage.

▶ **Avoid specific situations** that trigger your attitude of comparing, such as going to the gym after a disagreement with your husband.

▶ **The decision** to stop comparing is yours to make. Your behavior won't change unless you take steps to do so. Usually, the first step will be the realization that this attitude is wrong.

> *Let each one examine his own work, and then he will have rejoicing in himself alone, and not in another.*
> Galatians 6:4, NKJV

question

▼

Why does he want to control what the two of you watch on TV?

There are few things as frustrating as watching a program, getting engrossed in the subject or the plot, and then missing the most important part—the few seconds that come immediately after the commercials' end. Television programmers know you want to see that conclusion to the previous scene's cliff-hanger, and structure their ads so that at the very least, you will watch part of the last commercial. Knowing that boredom is the root cause of channel surfing helps you understand why he wants to take control of the remote.

answer

▼

Men's brains are stimulated by sight, and their attention is captured by visual imagery. Women, however, are interested in relationships. You probably don't get interested in a program where you don't connect with the characters, while your husband has no problem following three football games at a time just by changing back and forth between channels. You prefer to watch one game, get to know the players better, and be able to know who wears what number jersey.

Aside from boredom, your husband may choose to change channels because he doesn't like the subject matter of the program you are watching. See if this is the case. Discuss his objections and your reasons for watching the program, and then decide together how you can both be happy. Always remember that a virtual-reality relationship is not as important as the real relationship between husband and wife.

The good news is, if you remember you are watching television together so that you can spend time together, the program you watch will become secondary. And if you know that he isn't channel surfing just to irritate you, you will be able to relax and relinquish the remote.

worth thinking about

▶ **When being physically** close to each other is your focus, it won't really matter what you watch together. Get comfy, snuggle up, and enjoy.

▶ **Avoid the commercial** trap by recording your programs in advance or by using prerecorded movies. You can cut the cost of renting by borrowing from friends or your local library.

▶ **Women often think** of commercial breaks as the time to get up and do something useful or productive. Use this time instead to mute the sound and talk to your husband for a few minutes.

> *He wants each of you to learn to control your own body in a way that is holy and honorable.*
> 1 Thessalonians 4:4, NCV

question

He wants to buy *what?*

Your husband's idea of a great deal and yours will probably differ, particularly, it seems, as the price gets higher and higher. It can be a real shock to hear your husband get excited about buying something that is important to him but on the bottom of your list of must-haves. Having a plan in place before the occasion arises is the best way to avoid conflict over differences of opinion in purchasing priorities.

answer

Being able to combine your goals and his into a cohesive unit that benefits your marriage and your family is probably not going to come easily for either one of you. You each have your own opinions, insecurities, and goals as individuals, and they may not always cause you to make the best decision for each other.

Formulating some guidelines will help you through the process. Knowing in advance how much each of you can spend without discussing it with your spouse gives each of you some freedom and independence. Deciding together on the big-ticket items will draw you together as a couple as you define your reasons for and against the purchase.

Very often the ticket price is not the only cost. Consider licensing, insurance, membership fees, travel time, learning costs, and time away from your family when making a purchase.

The important thing to remember is that no matter how crazy an idea your husband seems to have regarding a purchase, he has his reasons. Determine to listen carefully to him as he explains the potential benefits of the purchase to your marriage and your family, and respectfully consider what he says. The next time a crazy idea comes up, it might be yours, and you would want him to hear you out.

worth thinking about

▶ Few decisions have to be made on the spur of the moment. If you can't come to some agreement, then at least agree to put off the decision for the time being.

▶ Salespeople can often put unrealistic and untruthful pressure on you to buy now or lose the deal. Always go together when making a purchase where pressure to buy may be an issue.

▶ Knowing where you stand financially will help you both make wiser decisions. Know your bank balance and debt amounts, as well as monthly commitments already made. Don't overextend yourselves.

> Is there anyone here who, planning to build a new house, doesn't first sit down and figure the cost so you'll know if you can complete it?
> Luke 14:28, THE MESSAGE

question

Why does he give you advice when you don't ask for it?

Often when you share an experience with your husband, you might forget that he is in solution mode while you are in sharing mode. Your intentions are not always to solicit a solution—sometimes you just want to be able to talk it through. It will help you structure your discussions if you realize that he isn't trying to cut you off but that he wants to deal with what he views as a possible problem and get on to something else.

answer

When your husband hears what he thinks is a problem, his brain may stop listening to the rest of the conversation as it races to find a way to fix the situation. You want to let him know how you felt, and he wants to know how to stop the hurt you experienced. You want to relive the experience, savor the parts that went well, and seek insight into how to avoid the part that made you feel bad.

Most men enjoy the cerebral exercise of evaluating options, considering choices, and then deciding on the best course of action. You both want to make the best decision possible given the circumstances. However, the ways you approach a problem may be different. This is no flaw in your brain, just as it is not a flaw in your husband's brain. It is the way God created you, because together, you are better.

Knowing that your husband is doing what he thinks you want him to do—fix the problem and give some answers—will help you as he gives advice you didn't ask for. Understanding that he isn't criticizing your handling of the situation, but rather that he just wants to be able to help you avoid a similar situation in the future, will help you consider what he is saying as helpful information. He really doesn't like to see you get hurt, and he does care about what you are thinking and feeling.

worth thinking about

▶ Communicate to your husband when you want to just talk and you aren't specifically looking for advice. The time will come when you will want his input, and you don't want to discourage his willingness to help.

▶ Because your husband really does want to help you, make sure you include him in some situations where you do want some advice.

▶ There is nothing wrong with letting him know you have already thought the problem through and have a solution, but you would still like to hear his opinion.

> *Listen to counsel and accept discipline,*
> *that you may be wise the rest of your days.*
> Proverbs 19:20, NAS

question

How do you deal with his lack of emotion?

Men often give the perception that they either lack emotion or just don't care enough about the situation to show emotion. The truth is that men show feelings in different ways and for different reasons than women do. You can deal with your perception of his lack of passion or sentimentality by knowing that he does feel emotion but that he will demonstrate it in a different way than you will.

answer

When considering your perception of your husband's lack of emotion, you may be referring to his apparent lack of tears or compassion. Society is part of the reason men show their emotions differently than women do—they are raised to be strong, silent types. Boys are not supposed to cry. Women tend to show emotion over relationship issues, while men tend to show emotion when they are hurting or see someone they love hurting. In many cases, your husband will not cry, but that doesn't mean he is hurting any less inside.

You can change how you expect your husband to show emotion by accepting that he isn't wrong just because he doesn't react the way you do. Understanding your husband's different moods and responses to situations will enable you to detect a display of emotion that you might otherwise have missed. Becoming quiet or wanting to be alone is one way many men deal with times of emotional upset. Respecting his need to work through his feelings as he sees fit is one way to help him through this time.

On the other hand, when your husband is celebrating a joyous moment, he may want to spend it with as many people as possible, so be prepared to share your good news with others. Know that as soon as he has shared his joy with as many people as will listen, he will be glad to spend some time alone with you to celebrate together, in private.

worth thinking about

▶ **For many men**, good news is a reflection on them as a person and on their success, and is to be shouted from the highest rooftop. Plan a party, put on a smile, and share your husband's joy.

▶ **Grief can carry** a lot of guilt, and it is therapeutic to be able to show those emotions and get past them. If your husband struggles in this area, encourage him that it is safe to open up to you and express what he is feeling.

▶ **Some men may** hide their emotions deep inside for fear of being ridiculed. Let your husband know that you won't laugh at him if, for example, he cries over a sappy movie, and then stick to your promise.

> *Those who do right should be glad and should rejoice before God; they should be happy and glad.*
> Psalm 68:3, NCV

43

question
▼
Why can't he read your mind?

While it may seem incomprehensible to you that your husband doesn't understand what you are trying to say and what you really mean, you need to understand that your mind is a mystery to him. The brain is compartmentalized into left and right brain sections in both male and female, but the male brain has less communication between the segments. As a result, unless you let him know how you think and how you arrive at your conclusions, your thought processes will seem like a maze to him.

answer
▼

Because of the additional communication in your brain between the left and right lobes, you are able to multifocus more easily than your husband can. This translates into your being able to talk on the phone, watch television, and know what the kids are doing in the next room. It also explains a phenomenon commonly known as "selective hearing."

If your discussions often end in tears or accusations, or if you tend to demonstrate fluctuations in mood or behavior, your husband may be reluctant to know how your mind works. Strive for rational thinking and logical processes of arriving at conclusions. Do your homework on a particular topic that you don't know much about so you can discuss it with him. Ask him to clarify any of his thoughts that confuse you.

In order for your husband to understand you and be able to anticipate your decisions, you need to share with him in an atmosphere of trust and vulnerability. Encourage him to share with you as well so that you can grow together as a couple. Being able to read each other's minds should be a process that draws you together into unity.

worth thinking about

▶ **Remind your husband** that you can find his misplaced car keys because of being able to multifocus and that you appreciate his ability to be able to singularly focus on a specific task that requires extra concentration.

▶ **Your husband's** more focused approach is critical when it comes to decision making. Share with each other the benefits of arriving at the same conclusion from two different directions as confirmation of the correct decision.

▶ **Check your** communication style, and make changes if you see that you are being too abstract in how you say things. One way to do that is to record your conversation and then listen to it to see if you understood what you were trying to say.

> Lord, *you know my heart.*
> *You see me and test my thoughts.*
> Jeremiah 12:3, NLT

question

How do public displays of affection show your love?

Public displays of affection—PDAs—have undergone a radical transition in recent years. Where once it would have been inappropriate even for a married couple to hold hands as they walked down the street, now those visible demonstrations of your love are appropriate and even encouraged. Showing your feelings toward your husband in public would, of course, normally be limited to nonsexual signals.

answer

Showing your intimate relationship outside your private surroundings shows your commitment to each other and can set a good example for others as you demonstrate your love and intimacy in a tasteful, conservative manner. You can show others that love is about feeling comfortable with each other and your relationship so that you don't have to go to extremes of behavior.

Public displays of affection require more self-control than a private display would, and they will encourage you to act respectfully and responsibly because you know others are watching. You can demonstrate to your children how to show love in public through holding hands, chaste kissing, and appropriate touching, setting guidelines that will aid them in their own dating relationships.

Showing love in public may be a huge step outside your comfort zone for you, and it may even take more courage for you to show your husband your love. This can be good, especially if he knows you are doing this because he likes it.

If your husband isn't comfortable with PDAs, you might begin with holding hands and touching more in the privacy of your home or your car when you travel together. You can also begin by talking with him about his reluctance, and reassuring him that your desire is to show your love for him to him and others tastefully.

worth thinking about

► **Public displays** of affection are meant to reestablish and reconnect throughout the time when you are not alone.

► **PDAs can be** part of foreplay in a nonsexual way. Touch is important to your sexual intimacy, and PDAs can begin the process of stimulating your senses.

► **Public displays** of affection should be appropriate to the occasion, and you should never want to make anyone around you uncomfortable, especially your husband. When it comes to PDAs, less is better than too much, and you shouldn't draw attention to yourself or away from someone else.

> *Live a lover's life, circumspect and exemplary,*
> *a life Jesus will be proud of.*
> Philippians 1:10, THE MESSAGE

question

Why does he forget dates that are important to you?

Men tend to focus on the event, while women tend to focus on the date itself. This difference in their focus will also extend to differences in perspective, including the importance of dates and events. Your husband treasures you and the good memories associated with the special dates in your lives, dates such as your anniversary, the births of your children, and your own birthday. As such, he is much more interested in the fact that it happened, not the details of when. Rejoice in the fact that your husband wants to celebrate these special times with you, and don't fret if he gets a date wrong.

answer

Many times what happens in a marriage is that because the date itself can be more important to you than to him, you both might fall into the pattern of your having to remind him of upcoming events. While this can reduce stress, it can also backfire if you forget to remind him. He is more likely to not remember the date if you have been acting as his personal calendar keeper. When he does forget, if you can acknowledge that it is not because he is trying to irritate you, then you will not put pressure on him to remember the date.

Your husband does not intentionally forget the dates that are important to you, and if you focus on the event and not just the date, you will be able to enjoy your celebrations. Taking your attention off the date and putting it on the event will allow you to celebrate the event for what it is—a memorial to a good memory. The Bible says that God created memorials so that you could remember and teach your children about the good things He has done for you.

worth thinking about

▶ **Once the date** itself is not the focus, you will be willing and able to celebrate anytime. A joyful celebration a week early or a day late is better than one planned out of obligation on the date of the celebration.

▶ **You can alternate** who is responsible for arranging celebrations. For example, you might choose to be responsible for wedding anniversaries in even years, and he can be responsible for the ones in the odd years.

▶ **Celebrations are not** meant to be competitions. The fact that you go all out for your husband's birthday and he remembers yours a week late doesn't mean he loves you any less than you love him.

> *Those who feared the LORD spoke to one another, and the LORD listened and heard them; so a book of remembrance was written before Him for those who fear the LORD and who meditate on His name.*
> Malachi 3:16, NKJV

question

How often should you pray for your husband?

answer

I have not stopped
thanking God for you.
I pray for you constantly.

Ephesians 1:16 NLT

46 question

How do you get him to give up that piece of clothing?

People often judge you by what you are wearing, particularly if it is inappropriate for the occasion. For whatever reason, men often develop a sentimental attachment to clothing beyond its usefulness. This attachment could be to a college jacket, a pair of gym shorts, or comfy slippers. Most often this attachment is because of familiarity, memories, or because an item of clothing fits comfortably.

answer

Respect for the reason why your husband is attached to a particular piece of clothing extends to respect for your husband. Often a college letter jacket will be an important piece of clothing your husband may want to keep because it reminds him of his carefree days in college and also makes him feel young. You can respect those memories and feelings associated with the jacket by suggesting that you have it professionally mounted in a wall case or picture frame.

If the piece of clothing is so worn out it is either completely nonfunctional or is embarrassing to be seen in because of its condition, be willing to talk to your husband about why he wants to wear it. If it is because he finds it comfortable, offer to go shopping with him or for him to find for a suitable replacement. Discard the old piece only after a satisfactory replacement is found.

If he has attached sentimental reasons to a piece of clothing because someone special gave it to him, and particularly if the article is not serving its intended purpose, talk with your husband about what the article represents about the person who gave it to him. Offer to find a picture of your husband with the giver and the gift to display. If this is agreeable, discard the worn-out gift and remember the giver through the picture.

worth thinking about

▶ **If your husband** insists on wearing a particular piece of old clothing in public, talk to him. Don't throw out anything that belongs to him without first obtaining his approval.

▶ **If there is something** he is not ready to give up right now, then wait. If he agrees, pack it in a box, put the date on it, and agree to check it again in a year.

▶ **Just because** the article is old doesn't mean it needs to be ratty. If he really wants to wear it, check into having it professionally repaired. If it is beyond repair, consider taking part of it and incorporating that into another piece of clothing or maybe even framing it or adding it to a quilting project.

> *Life is more than food,*
> *and the body is more than clothes.*
> Matthew 6:25, NCV

question

Why does he act like he's the most valuable player?

Your husband wants to be the leader in your home and your marriage, and as such, it can be easy for him to think he is the most important person. This is probably not his intention, however, and you can change any misconceptions you both have by remembering that you both are on the same team. There is a difference between being the leader in your home and being the center of everything, and the main difference is in attitude.

answer

Most people want to feel they are important to someone, and your husband is no different. As a result, he may tend to overpower your relationship and conversations. As a man, his voice will tend to be louder and his physical presence more overbearing than yours, and you may interpret that to mean he has a he-man attitude. In most cases, however, when you are able to understand that his physical presence is not intended to overwhelm you but to protect and nurture you, then you will be able to see past the deeper voice and bigger muscles to a man who wants to show others—and you—that he is worthy of you.

Sit down with your husband and talk about your perceptions and concerns. You can reassure him that you are not trying to diminish his position as leader of your home or emasculate him in any way. Make sure he knows just how important he is to you. Your world really does revolve around him—he is your husband, after all. And his world revolves around you, his wife. Let him know that you understand you are different physically as well as emotionally and that you don't expect him to act like you. In talking with him, you will show your love by your desire to address an issue that concerns you and to show him that you really want to work this out to benefit both of you.

worth thinking about

▶ For every most valuable player in any sport, there are always those unnamed players who make the MVP look good. You are one of the players who make your husband look good.

▶ Consider whether your perception of his attitude really stems from your own desire to be the center of your marriage. God designed marriage to be a partnership, where the husband is the leader.

▶ If your husband really does have an attitude problem and is willing to acknowledge that, take small steps toward making positive changes.

> *Those who are last now will someday be first, and those who are first now will someday be last.*
> Matthew 20:16, NCV

question

How is his need for encouragement different from yours?

As a woman, your need for encouragement likely revolves around how you are treating others, how others feel about you and the ones you love, and how you can improve others' lives in some way. Your husband's need for encouragement is centered on how others perceive him, on how his work defines him, and on how he fails or succeeds in accomplishing specific tasks he has set for himself. In essence, you are encouraged through emotional connections, while your husband is encouraged through accomplishment.

answer

As a result, your husband not only needs to know he is moving forward and developing as a person, he needs to see that in tangible ways. While you can be satisfied by feeling encouraged, your husband must see the results of the encouragement. This can often create a communication chasm as you each strive to feel encouraged in different ways.

Each person requires a different amount of encouragement to feel satisfied and fulfilled. Studies have shown that everyone needs daily affirmation that he is worthwhile and doing a good job. Although your husband may seem like the strong, silent type, he is no different; he needs that daily affirmation. Give you husband that emotional acceptance and support through your words, your actions, your thoughts, even your eyes.

You and your husband will demonstrate and receive encouragement in different ways, but this should not discourage you from continuing to find ways to give him the affirmation and uplifting that he needs.

worth thinking about

▶ **Ask your husband** if there are things he would like you to do, or not do, to express your encouragement. Sometimes his encouragement deficiency may be because he doesn't recognize your words or actions.

▶ **Your husband needs** to know that you think he is doing a good job, especially when those around him are saying something different.

▶ **You can help** replenish your husband's encouragement quota by being quick to praise and slow to criticize. Assessing his daily activities will help you see if there is something happening in his work or family relationships that may be draining his encouragement levels.

> *Let us consider one another in order to stir up love and good works.*
> Hebrews 10:24, NKJV

question
▼
Why does he need you more than you need him?

Men and women have different strengths based on gender, and these strengths are not all physical. Add to that the differences resulting from talent, experience, and cultural expectations, and the result is that you and your husband are a unique combination. Dependence on each other grows in the process of recognizing these abilities and strengths and then applying them to your marriage relationship. In that process, you will see that you share a mutual need for each other.

answer
▼

It can be frustrating when you feel that everything revolves around you and relies on you to be accomplished. In many marriages, the situation is a result of the pervasive Wonder Woman. As a woman, God created you to care for and nurture your husband and your family. Unfortunately, society has added to the growing list of accomplishments expected of women, such as holding down a career, raising a perfect family, and always looking sexy, no matter how tired you might be.

It might seem that your husband wouldn't be able to manage his life without you, but the truth is, he needs your input and ideas more than he needs you to do the laundry. He needs your love more than he needs you to find his car keys or cook his meals. He needs you to support him in his decisions more than he needs you to work to support the family. You need your husband for the emotional strength and balance he can provide, and to help you illustrate what a loving marriage relationship looks like.

Your husband views your ability to relate with people and build relationships as the other side of his building-and-solving coin. You and your husband are partners, and you need each other to accomplish God's plan in your lives.

worth thinking about

▶ **There are many** things your husband could hire someone to do for him, such as cooking and cleaning. He doesn't need you for those things.

▶ **Your husband** is a solver; you are a relationship builder. Solutions without relationship are just orders. He needs you to develop those relationships with others.

▶ **You can help** your husband by identifying a weakness and turning it into a strength. For example, if he tends to lose things a lot, help him organize with key hooks, colored hangers, see-through storage boxes, and open storage spaces.

> The LORD God said, "It is not good that man should be alone; I will make him a helper comparable to him."
> **Genesis 2:18**, NKJV

50

question

Why does he want to have the last word?

Men are wired differently from women. Their brains tend to view a problem as a situation itching for an answer. Women use questions to get information and build deeper relationships. When you talk to him about a problem, he is in solution mode. The end of the conversation comes when the solution is reached. Understanding these differences in the way men and women communicate will help you understand why your husband wants to have the last word.

answer

There is an old joke that the husband can be sure to always have the last word in any conversation, so long as the last words are "yes, dear." However, your husband always agreeing with what you want cannot simply resolve most discussions or disagreements. While this may sound like a good idea, after a time you will find there are many unresolved issues, and even some bad decisions being made. Because let's face it, women don't always have the right answer any more than men do.

Ask questions in order to gain understanding of your husband's point of view. If your husband thinks you are asking questions only in order to determine if he is making the right decision, then he will view this as a sign of disrespect. When you are truly interested in how your husband makes decisions, then he will want to share the details of that decision.

You can have more confidence in your husband's decisions and understand better how he thinks and arrives at his conclusions by being willing to let him explain his point of view. Don't make your husband defend his position, and you will find he will be open to listening to your ideas before he makes his final decision.

worth thinking about

▶ **If your discussions** tend to become never-ending, consider letting the situation rest for a while. Come back to him a few hours or a day later and repeat back your understanding of the conversation.

▶ **If you really** don't understand the direction he wants to take, repeat back what you understand, and ask him if this is correct. Allow him to explain again to clarify any discrepancies between his intended message and your understanding.

▶ **If you don't agree** with him, determine if his decision is life-changing. If it is, suggest you pray together for direction before making the final decision.

> *I send [my word] out, and it always produces fruit. It will accomplish all I want it to, and it will prosper everywhere I send it.*
>
> Isaiah 55:11, NLT

51 question

Why doesn't he ask your opinion?

If your husband didn't realize it before you were married, he is learning there are fundamental differences in the way men and women communicate. In this busy world, communication can fall by the wayside, and it can be easy to make decisions independently without much consultation with each other. When that happens, you may think he isn't asking for your opinion because he doesn't value it.

answer

The fact is that you both have probably succumbed at some point to a high-pressure sales pitch, a spur-of-the-moment decision, or some form of peer pressure. Recognizing that choosing to make decisions together is a sign of strength rather than weakness will help both of you resist the urge to make independent decisions.

Men tend to view a problem from the big-picture angle, where the question really is what information is needed to get to the facts. A woman, on the other hand, wants to know how the solution affects the people she cares about. Precisely because of these differences, you both make valuable contributions to the decision-making process and your opinion can be just as valid as his.

Perhaps the real issue is not that he doesn't ask your opinion but that you think he doesn't take it into consideration, since he appears to follow through on his decision regardless of your input. If this is the case, talk to him about your concerns. Ask him to remind you of a time when he incorporated your input into his decision. This will remind you both that your thoughts and ideas are important.

It may be easier to make changes by starting small. Remember to ask his opinion on various topics, and encourage him to ask your opinion as well. When you are both interested and informed about what is going on in each other's lives, you will both be more likely to open up to each other and welcome input.

worth thinking about

▶ **Encourage your husband** to ask your opinion by doing your research on the major things that come up, such as mortgages, the housing market, vehicles, and retirement.

▶ **If you find yourselves** making major decisions independent of each other, decide you will pray together before making the next decision.

▶ **If he doesn't** follow your suggestion, don't allow it to drive a wedge between you. Instead, remember this isn't a competition between you, it is a partnership.

> *Everyone who asks receives; he who seeks finds; and to him who knocks, the door will be opened.*
> Matthew 7:8, NIV

question

▼

How can conversation strengthen your connection with him?

It can be difficult to give or receive encouragement when you feel emotionally detached from those around you. You feel connected to your husband because of what you share, not because of how you differ. You and your husband are a team, striving to finish a race. As a team, there is no absolute winner, and you both win when you cross the finish line together. Conversation is the starting point, and your emotional connection to each other is the finish line.

answer

▼

True conversation is the sharing of thoughts and ideas, which fulfills a need and reinforces your relationship. You can feel connected through your daily conversations as you accomplish specific tasks, such as deciding who will have time to go to the dry cleaners or what you will have for supper. Another way to connect is through words of love and endearment, where you affirm your relationship with each other.

Deeper conversation can draw you closer in your relationship as you open yourselves up to each other in a more intimate way. Sharing dreams and fears creates a vulnerability, allowing you the opportunity to reassure each other of your care and commitment.

Showing support through a tough time by holding each other close will say far more than words ever could. Holding hands, hugging, even a pat on the back can all be ways of showing that you are physically and emotionally available. Even if you are in a crowd, you can communicate with each other through a glance or a smile.

The desire to feel in unity with your husband is natural. God created marriage to be an intimate relationship between you, where you support and build up each other through your words and actions. Making sure you invest the time and energy needed to create that intimacy will reap many rewards for your marriage.

worth thinking about

▶ **Feeling connected** is especially important when one of you is feeling particularly drained by a situation.

▶ **Emotional connection** doesn't just happen because you get married. It requires an investment of time and energy as you each seek to find ways to uplift and edify the other.

▶ **Sometimes this feeling** of being connected and in unity surfaces when you least expect it. Look for unusual ways to show your husband that you are in the race with him, to the finish.

Keep your eyes on Jesus, who both began and finished this race we're in.
Hebrews 12:2, THE MESSAGE

question

▼

How can you have a real conversation with him?

Men and women define *conversation* in different terms. If you were to ask your husband how you could have a real conversation with him, he would argue that you have real conversations every time you talk. To him, conversation is the exchange of information and finding solutions. You define real conversation as getting to the heart of the matter, establishing and deepening your emotional connection to the other person. Knowing this difference in expectations will help you better understand how he communicates.

answer

▼

For you, a real conversation will include sharing your feelings, which is something your husband will tend to avoid. Boys are raised to keep their emotions inside, and therefore many men find it difficult to put their feelings into words. When you share, you make yourself vulnerable to the other person, and most men are not willing to take that chance.

The first step to deepening the content of your conversations with your husband is to make talking to you a safe place for him. He needs to know that you will listen with respect, you will not ridicule or belittle his feelings or thoughts, you will not share what he says with anyone else unless he says it is okay, and you will give advice only when asked.

For your husband, respect and love go very much hand in hand. Respecting his feelings and his decisions will strengthen your relationship with him. As he opens up in deeper conversation, encourage him by listening carefully and respectfully.

Being able to voice your true feelings to the one person in the world you should feel safe with is liberating, and it is the very essence of what God designed the marriage relationship for.

worth thinking about

▶ **If your husband** has difficulty opening up to you, try asking questions that require more than a yes or no answer.

▶ **Don't introduce** more than one topic in a conversation so that you don't get off on a tangent to avoid a difficult topic.

▶ **Start small.** Save difficult topics for times when you both have energy to devote to them. Allow each other to speak openly, pausing after two or three sentences, giving each other the chance for feedback, and allowing each other to respond.

▼

Be gracious in your speech. The goal is to bring out the best in others in a conversation, not put them down, not cut them out.

Colossians 4:6, The Message

question

How do you keep your conversations alive and exciting?

It can be easy to fall into a pattern of talking with your husband in which you address only the immediate needs of the moment and put out the fires around you. The harder thing is to solve the daily problems and address those things that need to be accomplished while maintaining and enhancing the intimacy of your marriage relationship. You can avoid just talking and make your conversation more interesting by keeping the negative to a minimum while you focus on your husband's strengths.

answer

Most people are always interested in talking about what interests them, and your husband is no different. Make it a point to bring up his interests, encouraging him to make time for them on a regular basis. Discuss common interests, and seek new information about those things you both enjoy. Even a discussion where you have differing viewpoints can be exciting as you each share your opinions and understanding without the pressure of having to change each other's mind.

Your husband will be excited to hear what God is accomplishing in your faith walk with Him. Share your struggles and victories with him, and encourage him to share with you. Enjoy even the smallest of accomplishments with each other. You never know when you will be able to glean a tidbit of information from something your husband has already gone through that can be applied to a situation you are currently facing.

Developing good listening skills will allow you both to enter into the discussion, offer positive and uplifting comments, and still challenge each other's thinking skills. You both will soon experience an overall feeling of excitement about your time together.

worth thinking about

▶ Save in-depth conversations for when you aren't tired or distracted so that you both can contribute and receive.

▶ To create and maintain the excitement, don't just talk. Interact with each other in nonverbal ways as well, such as holding hands when the topic is serious, tickling when the topic is funny, or using hand motions when telling a story.

▶ Too often conversation becomes a time of complaining or blaming. Make sure that any time you discuss a serious topic, you face each other, offer solutions, and don't assign blame.

> *Anxiety in the heart of man causes depression, but a good word makes it glad.*
> Proverbs 12:25, NKJV

question

How do you show respect that won't be misinterpreted?

Sometimes it may seem as if you and your husband are speaking entirely different languages. You think you are telling him you respect him, but he misinterprets what you say. Your husband does read between the lines of what you tell him, even if it seems he doesn't. His interpretation of what you are saying may not be what you intended. When that happens, it is important to speak to him in a language he will understand.

answer

Your husband can easily confuse how you speak to him with how he understands what you are saying. As a result, a question from you may sound like you are second-guessing him or trying to undermine his decision, when all you want is to understand what he is telling you. This doesn't mean you can never ask questions. However, your husband will know the difference between asking questions for understanding and asking questions to undermine or erode his confidence. You can begin by repeating back your understanding of what he just said, and allow him to clarify any misunderstandings immediately.

Show him respect by not speaking negatively about him, by showing solidarity with his decisions, by speaking positively about your relationship with each other, and by encouraging him in his career and friendships. You and your husband can clear up many misconceptions by talking about your concerns when they happen. While he may be resistant to talking openly at first, he will be more willing to talk if he sees that you really want his input and that you aren't trying to assign blame.

Words are not the only way to show respect. Sometimes actions speak even louder, so pay attention to the small details of your marriage, and make sure that everything you say and do reflects well on him as husband.

worth thinking about

▶ **Before you fall** asleep tonight, tell your husband five ways he showed you today that he loves you. Recognizing his love for you shows that you respect how he does that.

▶ **Allow him to compliment** you sincerely, and accept those compliments graciously. He sees you as an expression of his ability to win and provide for a beautiful woman.

▶ **Putting his needs** before your own validates him and helps him feel better about himself, and sacrificial loving will help you feel even better about yourself.

> *Love suffers long and is kind; love does not envy; love does not parade itself, is not puffed up.*
> 1 Corinthians 13:4, NKJV

How can you help him be more dependable?

My eyes shall be upon the faithful of the land, that they may dwell with me; he who walks in a blameless way is the one who will minister to me.

Psalm 101:6, NAS

56

question

How can you show him
honor through your words?

For your husband, honor and respect are closely related.
He will feel loved only when he believes he is honored
and respected. *Respect* is your attitude, while *honor* is
the outward demonstration of that respect. The old saying "Imitation is the highest form of flattery" is true for
showing honor as well—you honor the person you imitate when that imitation is done with sincerity.

answer

Honor without respect is hollow. Honor is shown
through your words and attitude when your husband is
present, and also through what you say and do when he
is not. One of the best ways to honor him through your
words is to be consistent in what you say whether he is
standing next to you or not.

Another way you honor your husband is by approaching
a decision in the same way he would. When others view
your authority in a decision as being the same as your
husband's, you create the impression of unity and
strength. As his wife, you represent your husband in all
your daily contacts. Treating others well in how you
speak to them will cause them to think well of you and
your husband.

You can show honor to your husband by standing in for him when he is not available. This could be in disciplining the children or in dealing with a customer or creditor. Consistency is the key to successfully honoring your husband. Tone of voice and body language can be more important than your actual words. Make sure that all three are in line with one another so that your husband and others will be able to hear not only what you are saying but what you mean.

Sincere compliments and positive words are sometimes rare occurrences. Choosing to honor your husband every day through what you say will cause him to feel better about himself, you, and your marriage.

worth thinking about

▶ **If you are having** a discussion, avoid using words like *never* or *always*. These words usually exaggerate and are rarely true. Your goal should be to build up your husband and your marriage.

▶ **Build up** your husband in front of others. Save your discussion for later when you are alone.

▶ **Don't joke** about him in public unless you both have agreed the incident was funny and that it's okay to share it with others.

> *Her husband is greatly respected when he deliberates with the city fathers.*
> Proverbs 31:23, THE MESSAGE

57 question

When is silence the best response?

Determining when not to speak is one of the most difficult lessons to learn in a marriage. You got married so you could spend more time together and share your most intimate thoughts and dreams with your husband, and now you need to figure out when to back off and let him have some silence. The art of knowing when to talk and when not to is something you can learn, and it will reap many rewards for you and your marriage.

answer

A person's mind can absorb only a certain amount of information before it needs to stop to process. You might infer that your husband is not interested, and this may be the furthest thing from the truth. He might simply be tired or distracted with his own thoughts. Bear in mind that your husband may get overwhelmed occasionally and that you can allow him the time to recover before you start another conversation.

Being quiet doesn't mean you don't have input. Not every thought you have needs to be expressed, and indeed, not every thought should be expressed. If you sense your husband is physically or emotionally weary, save the serious discussion and big decision until he is ready to deal with them. Always offer a solution if you are discussing a problem. If time is short, don't bring up a major topic. Wait until you both have more time.

If you feel your husband has made a bad decision, don't assign blame. Your husband knows if he made a mistake, and he doesn't need you telling him "I told you so."

The Bible says that you should use only words that encourage and build up the person you are speaking to. When that person is your husband, you will find that you are helping him become a better person.

worth thinking about

- ▶ **You will never** have to take back words you didn't speak. If you wonder whether you should say something, wait five minutes. If it still needs to be said, do so with love and tact.

- ▶ **When you** and your husband talk, sometimes staying quiet will allow him to get an issue off his chest. Remember, he isn't asking for advice. He just needs to speak it and be done with it.

- ▶ **If you feel** the discussion is progressing to an argument, stop talking and call a time-out. Remind each other that the purpose of the discussion is not to argue, and that you are each other's best friends. Resume the discussion when you are both calmer.

> *Let no corrupt word proceed out of your mouth,*
> *but what is good for necessary edification,*
> *that it may impart grace to the hearers.*
> Ephesians 4:29, NKJV

question

How can you tell the truth without little white lies?

Your closest relationship is with your husband, and it is natural to want him to think the best of you. While it may seem like an innocent thing when you embellish a story to make it more interesting or to make yourself look better, the transition from exaggeration to lying can take place insidiously. Telling the truth builds trust, while lies can undermine the foundation of your marriage. You can tell the truth and still remain tactful by knowing that while the truth may sting, it never hurts when it is told with love as its motivation.

answer

While white lies may seem useful for softening the truth you are trying to convey, you can speak truthfully without having to resort to embellishments. One way is to tell the truth without elaborating on details. It's usually in the explaining of the facts where you can get yourself into trouble by saying too much.

Truth doesn't mean telling everything about a particular topic. You don't know everything, and even if you did, the person listening probably doesn't want to know all the facts. You can tell the truth in love by always finding at least two good things to say for each negative thing.

Sandwich the negative thing between the two good comments so that you begin and end on a positive note.

Communication is a fragile thread between you and your husband, and you don't want your husband to see you as someone who is so blunt that when he talks to you he will always be wounded. On the other hand, you want to be taken seriously, and you want him to believe what you are saying.

Consider your communication style, and make changes if you see white lies of any size creeping in. Your intentions may be for the best, but others won't judge you by your intentions. They will judge you by what you say and do. Sometimes not offering an opinion will be the best way to show your love.

worth thinking about

▶ **If your husband** asks your opinion and you can't find anything good to say, don't say anything at all.

▶ **If you don't** know how to answer without hurting or being forced into a lie, try this: "That's a good question. What do you think?"

▶ **"I don't know"** is a good answer. There is nothing wrong with admitting you don't have an opinion or any knowledge on the topic being discussed.

> *Whoever of you loves life and desires to see many good days, keep your tongue from evil and your lips from speaking lies.*
> Psalm 34:12–13, NIV

question

How do you know when to share a confidence with him?

Within your circle of friends and acquaintances, some-one is bound to offer to share a tidbit of information with you if you promise not to tell anyone else. You can know which confidences to share with your husband by knowing in advance the situations that are important for him to know about and the ones that aren't. Talking to your husband about the general circumstances where you will each expect to share confidences is the key to solving the dilemma before it happens.

answer

Talking about this situation before it becomes an issue will strengthen the trust between you and your husband. Trust is not fostered through secrets. This doesn't mean you have to tell him everything—some things are just not important enough to pass on.

There are several situations where you should let him know what is going on. You should share if the confidence involves someone he is close to or is in business with, or if what you heard would reflect badly on him.

Any time you are struggling with a problem or a decision, it is always appropriate to go to your husband. You can ask advice without divulging details. Most secrets are a way to control your opinion and actions, and confirming the truth or the completeness of the details will likely be difficult without breaking the confidence.

It is best not to have confidences you feel you can't share with your husband. Avoid situations where gossip is spread, or where you are likely to overhear or see something not intended for you. When you avoid even the appearance of being involved in the confidence, you can actually help the other people involved by being a neutral party, untouched by the secret. By not getting embroiled in the situation, you can be a better friend.

worth thinking about

▶ **No matter how** juicy the tidbit of information your friend wants to tell you, if she prefaces the statement with "Promise you won't tell anyone," that is your chance to tell her you don't keep secrets from your husband.

▶ **By all means** do not disclose proprietary secrets of your employer, particularly if you have signed a nondisclosure agreement.

▶ **There are** some secrets that are okay not to share, including arrangements for a surprise celebration, the gender of an unborn baby, or similar instances where the truth is the surprise.

The fruit of righteousness will be peace;
the effect of righteousness will be
quietness and confidence forever.
Isaiah 32:17, NIV

60

question

What is your husband's love language?

Entire books have been written on the subject of love languages, the expression of physical and relational love. The way you demonstrate your love for your husband will be different from the way you express your love for family or friends. But your love for your husband is not shown in only a physical way.

answer

There are five main ways to show love, each with its own variations and applications: *words, touch, time, service,* and *gifts*. Each person will understand love through one primary language of love, and many times there will be one or more secondary languages as well.

You can determine which language your husband better understands by considering how he tells you that he loves you. Many times people will use their own love language to communicate their feelings. Look at how he expresses love for family and friends.

Think about how he responds to your attempts to tell him you love him. If he responds more to spending time together than to gifts, you will know that time is at least one of his primary love languages.

Through this process, you may find you have been showing him love all along and that he did comprehend it. In this case, the process will have confirmed that for you and will allow you to concentrate your energies on what he responds to. Showing love is a natural response to the feelings of love and the deepening of your marriage relationship, and being able to receive and understand love is integral to the success of your marriage.

worth thinking about

- ▶ **If you aren't sure** which language your husband speaks, concentrate on each love language for one week at a time to see which ones he responds to.

- ▶ *Words* of love include affirmation and praise. *Touch* is not only about sex; it also includes holding hands, massage, and kissing. *Time* is choosing to spend time with each other instead of doing something else. *Service* is doing things for him such as carrying his briefcase to the car. *Gifts* includes things you buy or make, such as his favorite cookies.

- ▶ **If you struggle** with finding the language he understands, ask him about times when he felt especially loved, or ask how his family members showed love for one another.

> *I pray that you and all God's holy people will have the power to understand the greatness of Christ's love.*
> Ephesians 3:18, NCV

61

How can you show him love without involving sex?

While sex within the confines of marriage is a wonderful way to express your love and enhance your emotional connection with each other, it is not the only way to demonstrate your love for each other. There may be times in your marriage when sex is not practical or possible, such as during times of illness or when one of you is away from home. However, there are other ways to express your love and connection, and one way is by knowing how your husband understands love.

answer

Your husband may understand demonstrations of love differently than you do, and being willing and able to show him love that he understands will encourage him to connect with you emotionally as well as physically. Knowing his love language will help you know other ways besides sex to show your love.

Even if touch is your husband's primary love language, not all touch has to be sexual in nature or in outcome. Nonsexual touch and contact will be important in sustaining your marriage, particularly if either of you travels a lot or works a job that requires you to spend long periods of time apart. While not meant to replace sexual intimacy, physical togetherness can fill in the gaps between your intimate times together. A hand around your waist, an affectionate squeeze on your shoulder, hand in hand while watching TV or reading a book together, or even simply eye contact and a smile at the mention of a mutual memory.

Regardless of what your husband's primary and even secondary love languages are, you can still show love in other ways. Spending time together, presenting small gifts or tokens of your love to him, conversation, and doing special things for him are other methods of showing your love and affection.

worth thinking about

▶ **If your husband** spends a lot of time on his feet during the day, plan a special foot-washing session for him. Use warm scented water in a bowl or basin, have a warmed towel nearby to dry his feet, and use a peppermint or spice-scented lotion to rub his feet afterward.

▶ **Go to a little** extra effort and expense in planning and preparing a special meal for him. He will be thrilled that you cared enough to go to the trouble.

▶ **Remember to always** send him off with a hug, a kiss, and a smile, even if he's just going to the corner store for a newspaper.

> *This is how we know what love is: Jesus Christ laid down his life for us.*
> 1 John 3:16, NIV

question

How do you show him love when you are not together?

Today's business and corporate world often requires a great deal of travel, and it may seem difficult to express your love for your husband when you are separated by miles or even time zones. However, even if your husband comes home every night or works out of your home, you can still show your love when you are not physically in the same room. Many times all it takes is planning ahead so that you are prepared.

answer

Regardless of why you are not together or how long you will be apart, you can still let him know you miss him and you're looking forward to when he comes home again. Phone calls at convenient times during the day, particularly if one of you is out of town, allow you to catch up on what is going on at home and to reestablish your emotional connection with each other. Text messages, e-mails, and faxes, which tend to be less interruptive, can serve the same purpose, although nothing really replaces hearing the sounds of each other's voices.

If your husband has to travel, offer to pack his suitcase for him. Include a picture of the two of you together tucked into a jacket pocket. You can also include a hankie with a dab of your favorite perfume. When he unpacks his suitcase, he will be reminded of how much you love him and care for him.

Establishing a pattern of connecting with each other during the day will help you maintain this pattern even if one of you is out of town.

Setting aside time for each other before prolonged business travel will help to sustain your intimacy while you are apart.

worth thinking about

▶ If your husband travels on business, you can show your love by taking care of the house, your children, and yourself while he is gone. Pay the bills, deal with any issues that arise, and arrange your schedule so that day-to-day activities, such as laundry and housekeeping, are done before he gets home.

▶ Acting as if your husband were with you at all times shows love. Handling money responsibly when he is not with you shows not only love, but respect as well.

▶ Be glad to see him when he comes home, and arrange a special homecoming, even if he is only gone for the day. Wear a smile when you greet him, and he will want to come home sooner the next time!

Regarding life together and getting along with each other, you don't need me to tell you what to do. You're God-taught in these matters. Just love one another!

1 Thessalonians 4:9, THE MESSAGE

63

question

Why should you put love notes in his lunches?

A man will tend to want to come home to the place where he feels as if he's been missed, where he is valued and loved and needed. You may do a wonderful job of showing your love to your husband when he is with you. However, the time will come when one or both of you will need to leave and go to work. Putting love notes in his lunch will accomplish many positive things, including helping you stay connected, reminding him of good memories, and making him smile.

answer

Just the act of taking the time to put a short note in with his lunch will remind him of your connection with each other. Even if he has been having a bad day, it will bring a smile to his face as he remembers that you are waiting for him at home.

When your husband's friends see your expressions of love, it may well make them jealous and want the same kind of relationship. The Bible says that holy jealousy is a good thing. Your notes may encourage others to make changes in their lives to emulate your relationship with your husband.

A love note can be used to remind your husband of a particularly good memory you have. It can also thank him for something he did recently that touched you deeply. You may even use a love note to tell him something personal and intimate that you have not been able to verbalize.

A love note in your husband's lunch is another form of communion, which the Bible says is important between those who love God. Communion isn't limited to the act of eating together, but demonstrates agreement and love between you and others. You can remind your husband of your agreement and desire for intimacy through this form of long-distance communion.

worth thinking about

▶ **To make sure** the note isn't read by the wrong person, tuck it in between two items, such as his sandwich and cookies.

▶ **If your husband** doesn't take a lunch, you can tuck the note into his jacket or pants pocket.

▶ **Use these notes** to speak love to your husband, not to remind him to pick up milk on the way home. Keep the note short, to the point, and upbeat.

Let love and faithfulness never leave you;
bind them around your neck, write them
on the tablet of your heart.
Proverbs 3:3, NIV

question

How does controlling your tongue show your love?

Sometimes the hardest thing you might have to do is not to give your opinion or respond to something your husband has said, particularly if it is hurtful. Remember that you are not the one who needs to change your husband. That is God's job. Forcing your opinion or responding from anger will probably not accomplish anything except to escalate the situation. You can show your love for your husband through self-control and wisdom.

answer

There will be times when your husband will make a decision you don't agree with. You can ask him if he is willing to listen to your opinion. If he acknowledges that his mind is already made up, encouraging him to talk the decision through with you may reveal any problems that exist in the decision. Let him know that if he decides to rethink his choice, you are more than willing to talk to him about it.

Allegations or insinuations that are unkind are not your goal in marriage. Sometimes emotion will get the best of both of you and things will be said that shouldn't be. In this situation, it may be best to let the statements remain unanswered until you both cool down. Later, when you both are more calm and rational, discuss how the statements made you both feel. In many cases, words spoken on impulse tend to be exaggerations and don't accomplish anything. Be quick to apologize, and quicker to forgive.

If you and your husband have fallen into a pattern of taunting each other to get a response, discuss your concerns about your desire to have input without the hurt that often results from words spoken out of emotion. Wanting to build each other up and make your marriage stronger should be your goal, and being willing to make changes in how you talk to each other will be a big first step.

worth thinking about

▶ **The Bible says** that the tongue controls your thoughts and actions, like a rudder controls a ship. Check your speech to make sure it is leading you where you want to go.

▶ **Allowing some times** of silence in your conversations will give you both time to process the information before you feel pressured to start formulating a response.

▶ **Your not responding** in anger can be humbling for him as he realizes you are trying to change your behavior, and can set an example for him and others on ways to improve communication.

> *Take control of what I say, O Lord,*
> *and guard my lips.*
> Psalm 141:3, NLT

question

Why do you need more than words to show love?

There are many ways to show your love for your husband, and it is easy to get stuck in a pattern of how you show love. It is also easy for your words and actions to correspond with how you are feeling at the moment. However, love is not dependent on feelings or circumstances—love is a decision you make. And sometimes that decision may need to be made several times a day, perhaps even moment by moment.

answer

Unconditional love is one of the most difficult concepts to understand and demonstrate, and yet it is central to your marriage. Living an attitude of love goes far beyond words or actions.

You can live an attitude of love by deciding that your marriage is the most important relationship you are in, next to your relationship with God. When you are in a warm and loving relationship with God, it will be easy to emulate that love toward your husband. As you see how God treats you even when you are not perfect, you will understand that you can treat your husband with the same grace as you receive.

When comparing your relationship with God to your marriage, you will see that God uses words to tell you how much He loves you, but He also reinforces those words with actions. In your marriage, actions require an effort on your part and show that you are thinking about your husband.

Whenever your husband sees you invest time and energy in your relationship, he knows that your feelings toward him are important to you and your relationship. People do not tend to invest in things that are not important to them. What you invest in will grow, and the time and effort you put into your marriage will be noticed and appreciated by your husband.

worth thinking about

▶ You can find many ways to show your love for your husband without ever using the word *love*. In the Bible, the Song of Solomon is a love letter, and there has been much poetry, music, and other classic literature written that is full of ideas for declaring and showing love.

▶ Words are easy and thus can be hollow. Make sure your words and your actions line up with each other.

▶ Unconditional love is accepting your husband as he is, and trusting that God will make whatever changes need to be made.

> *We should love people not only with words and talk, but by our actions and true caring.*
> 1 John 3:18, NCV

question

question
▼

How do you help him understand it's okay to ask for directions?

answer
▼

Jacob sent Judah ahead to meet Joseph and get directions to the region of Goshen.

Genesis 46:28, NLT

66

question

How do you show your love through listening to him?

One of your husband's goals in your marriage is to develop a deeper and more trusting relationship with you, and one way he does this is through talking with you. When he talks, he is sharing a part of himself as he connects with you emotionally. He will probably feel vulnerable as he trusts you with his thoughts. You can show your love as you listen to him by letting him know that his thoughts and concerns are safe with you.

answer

When you talk together, you are telling your husband that this time is for him, that you are investing this time in your marriage, and that you value his input. As he shares his dreams and concerns, it is important that you allow him to verbalize his thoughts and give him the time he needs to express himself. If this is new for your husband, he may also need additional time to work through his thoughts as he talks.

Listening tells your husband that you are accepting him as he is and that you are interested in what he has to say. You can encourage him to share by asking questions if he appears to be struggling with the concept he wants to share with you. However, don't feel that every minute has to be filled with words. Allow some times of reflection for both of you.

Acknowledge what he is saying by nodding your head. If you see he is having a hard time expressing himself, touch his hand or put your arm around him to encourage him. Allow him a safe environment to express any emotion connected with what he is telling you. Maintain eye contact, and smile as you listen. The more you encourage him to share, the easier it will be for him.

worth thinking about

▶ **You can encourage** your husband to share his dreams and concerns by setting aside time for both of you to talk when you won't be interrupted. You can begin by telling him of one of your goals and by asking him to share his with you. This is not a time for debate. Allow him to share with you without contradicting or insisting on equal time.

▶ **If you both struggle** with where to start, begin with a good shared memory, or you can start with an individual good childhood memory.

▶ **While not all topics** of your conversation will be upbeat, you can change the tone by asking him how he would like to see some changes made.

> *Love GOD, your God, listening obediently to him, firmly embracing him.*
> Deuteronomy 30:20, THE MESSAGE

question

How do you honor him in the way you dress?

When you married your husband, you promised to be faithful to him with your body. You honor your husband in the clothes you wear by covering those body parts that are reserved for him, so as to not draw other men's eyes and by setting an example for other young women, including your daughters and, eventually, daughters-in-law. This does not require you to go about in sackcloth or baggy clothes; dressing tastefully tells others that you are cherished and desirable, while not drawing undue attention.

answer

The clothes you wear reflect a lot about you, including your personality, your attention to detail, your income, and the way you feel about your body. Choosing to wear clothes that are suitable for the occasion, tasteful in their design, and respectful of others is a challenge with today's revealing styles.

It can be easy to fall into a pattern of dressing according to what is comfortable, such as always wearing sweatpants and baggy shirts around the house. Consider the image you portray. Your husband and children should be worthy of a little extra effort, just as much as an employer is.

Even if your clothing budget does not include the latest styles, you can still dress in an honoring way by making sure your clothes are clean, in good repair, and appropriate to the occasion. Take extra care with your hair and makeup, and wear a smile.

What you wear reflects directly on your husband's ability to provide for his family and his good taste by marrying you. You don't prove to others that you are secure in your marriage by showing a lot of skin; you show it in your attitude toward others and your husband. The best thing you can wear to honor your husband is an agreeable attitude, a loving heart, and a smile.

worth thinking about

▶ When buying clothes, choose a store that has mirrors on all sides in the dressing room. Look at your outfit from all angles, and do not purchase anything that clings or rides up.

▶ Buy clothes that are comfortable and fit well. Choose colors and styles that flatter without drawing unnecessary attention to yourself.

▶ If you aren't sure if an outfit looks good on you, ask a friend whose wardrobe you admire for advice.

> *I want women to be modest in their appearance. They should wear decent and appropriate clothing and not draw attention to themselves by the way they fix their hair or by wearing gold or pearls or expensive clothes.*
> 1 Timothy 2:9, NLT

question 68

Why can fantasies cause problems?

The human mind was created with the ability to go beyond reality and into imagination and memory. Memory allows you to recall past lessons, avoid the same mistakes, and develop deeper relationships. Imagination is important to improving your situation and finding solutions to existing problems. There is nothing wrong with using this virtual-reality ability that your brain possesses, but living in this virtual reality can cause problems for you and for your marriage.

answer

There is nothing wrong with imagination. Taken to the extreme, however, imagination becomes fantasy, which can take over your life and your thinking. Many people get caught up in fantasies because they feel their lives are out of control, and fantasy is one thing they think they can control. However, these fantasies can cause an unrealistic view of real life by creating dissatisfaction as real life is compared to a dream life.

Spending a lot of time in your fantasy world may cause you to want to make your fantasies reality. Your actions should be based on right and wrong, not on your fantasy world.

The word *fantasy* can conjure up many pictures in your mind, but the most prevalent is probably sexual fantasy, which is quite often more common with men. While it may appear to be a harmless pastime, much like daydreaming, spending a lot of time in sexual fantasy can be detrimental to your marriage, your social skills, and your mental stability.

While your fantasy or your husband's fantasy may seem harmless at first, it can quickly take over your lives. Regardless of whether your husband or you struggle in this area, you can help each other break the hold that fantasy has over you. Together you are a formidable weapon against this attack on your marriage.

worth thinking about

▶ **If you struggle** with spending too much time avoiding your real life, try to figure out one thing you can change to make your real life more attractive.

▶ **You can develop** interests that use your imagination for productive uses, not just for escape. Take a class in painting, writing, or dancing to give yourself that creative outlet.

▶ **If your husband** struggles with fantasies, don't just brush it off as that's what all men do. Talk with him, discuss his concerns, and see what part you can take in helping him through this battle.

> *How long must I wrestle with my thoughts and*
> *every day have sorrow in my heart?*
> *How long will my enemy triumph over me?*
>
> Psalm 13:2, NIV

question

Why isn't it okay to look around at other men?

It can be very easy to convince yourself that looking at other men is a harmless pastime or that you are just proving to yourself that you have the best husband in the world. However, no matter how perfect your husband is, at some point you will inevitably see something about another man that you wish your husband had or did, creating dissatisfaction as you see defects in your husband you hadn't noticed before. Looking at other men will ultimately create problems in your marriage.

answer

If you find yourself looking at other men to compare your husband to them, ask yourself why you are doing this. Comparing always requires that one thing be diminished as the other is increased. This means that either your husband or the other man is going to fall short.

If you try to rationalize that looking doesn't hurt so long as you don't touch, consider that the man you are comparing your husband to may well be another woman's husband, and ask yourself if you want another woman looking at your husband that way. Consider how you would feel if you saw your husband looking at another woman. No matter how well you may think you are disguising your thoughts, your husband will feel as if he is inadequate in some way.

Remember that most adulterous affairs don't begin with an intentional act of infidelity. Most begin with "harmless" flirtation or looks. Affairs begin with at least one party looking for fulfillment or affirmation they are not receiving in their marriage.

Show your love and faithfulness to your husband better by completely avoiding looking at other men to compare them to your husband or to check out the competition. Prove your faithfulness by flirting only with him. Demonstrate your love by keeping your mind clear of sexual innuendos that are not directly related to him. Show him you know he is the best husband in the world by having eyes only for him when you are out in public.

worth thinking about

▶ **If you struggle** with "just looking," make it a point to avoid those places where you might be more likely to look at other men, such as the beach, the pool, or the gym.

▶ **Avoid dressing provocatively** when you go out so that you don't draw the glances of other men.

▶ **Talk to a trusted** friend if you think you have a problem with looking at other men. Ask her for help in choosing activities that don't put you in temptation's way.

Put all evil things out of your life: sexual sinning, doing evil, letting evil thoughts control you, wanting things that are evil, and greed.
Colossians 3:5, NCV

70 question

How do you deal with his looking at other women?

Contrary to popular opinion, looking at other women in a sexual or lustful way is not complimentary to you or to women in general. Because the eyes lead the body and the mind, and because men's brains are more stimulated through vision than any other sense, if your husband looks at other women in a sexual way, he is playing with fire. You can help him overcome this behavior by letting him know how it makes you feel, and sharing research that explains the dangers he is exposing himself to.

answer

Regardless of how strong your marriage is or how self-controlled your husband believes he is, looking at other women is bound to lead to temptation. Women are not sexual objects placed here for your husband's pleasure. You are the only woman he is to take pleasure in, and your commitment to your marriage is a way to show your love. Communicating that to him will make him aware of his behavior and its negative impact on your marriage.

You can begin by asking him what about other women makes him want to look at them. If he is comparing you to them, ask if there are any changes he would like you to make. Let him know that you want to meet his needs and that you are not in competition with these other women.

You can ask your husband to consider what his behavior is saying to other people about you and your marriage, and ask him how he would feel if other men looked at you or your daughter in that manner.

Regardless of the temptation set before him, your husband is an adult with control of his emotions and feelings. He should have eyes for no other woman besides you, as you should have eyes for no other man besides him.

worth thinking about

▶ **If you find** he struggles with situations where women are scantily clothed, avoid those situations. Remind him that as his wife, you are the one who deserves the looks he is passing around freely to other women.

▶ **There are many** ways to be faithful in your marriage, and unfaithfulness isn't manifested only in sexual contact. Faithfulness is an attitude that is made alive through action.

▶ **Do not encourage** your husband to look at other women through the movies or television programs you watch. Limit the amount of sexual content you are both exposed to, choosing more family-friendly programming.

> *I made a covenant with my eyes not to look lustfully at a girl.*
> Job 31:1, NIV

question

How do you deal with negative comments about your husband?

Most people make negative comments about other people because of some dissatisfaction in their lives, not because they want to change the person they are talking about. Being around negative people can cause you to dwell on their dissatisfactions, and may even cause you to become unhappy with some area of your own life. Be prepared to counter those negative comments and to offer positive solutions to offset the negativity.

answer

Your first reaction to hearing someone speak negatively about your husband may be anger. How dare they talk about the man you love like that! However, if you allow those comments to stew in your mind, particularly if you have been having a bad day yourself, you might just find yourself agreeing, at least to some degree, to the comments.

Resign yourself to knowing that at some point in your marriage, someone is going to say something against your husband to you. Know in advance that no matter how close to the truth the comments might be, your husband is not trying to do something that will harm you or your family. Tell the person you do not want to hear what he or she has to say, and/or simply walk away.

If the talk continues, or it is a troubling topic, go to your husband and tell him what you have heard. Allow him to explain the truth about the situation. The next time you are confronted with what you now know is a lie, you will be able to set the record straight with the facts.

When you show your husband and others that you and he are in agreement, that you are honest and truthful with each other, and that you trust each other implicitly, there will be no opportunity for negative comments to drive a wedge between you and your spouse.

worth thinking about

▶ **Your husband needs** to know you will not believe anything negative about him from someone else without proof and discussing it with him first. You need to know that he has your best interests at heart, and that together you are strong enough to withstand any attack.

▶ **Having an action plan** in place is always the best place to start. Discuss with your husband how any negative comments or gossip you hear about each other will be handled.

▶ **To avoid getting caught** in the gossip cycle, do not listen to or contribute to any negative discussion where the person who is the topic is not present.

> *Don't talk out of both sides of your mouth;*
> *avoid careless banter, white lies, and gossip.*
> Proverbs 4:24, THE MESSAGE

question

How can you show your
extended family that you
support your husband?

Apart from your husband, your relatives probably know
you better than anyone else does. It is not enough to be
behind him 100 percent; it must be evident to others
and to your husband. You do that through your words
and actions, through your body language and your attitude. Support for your husband can manifest itself in
different ways, but the best way to show that support is
to live it each and every day.

answer

Your extended family needs to see that you choose to
support your husband because it is the best thing for you
and for your marriage. Speaking positively about your
husband and his accomplishments is a good place to
start. Show them how much you support your husband
by not comparing him with other husbands, particularly
ones in your family circle.

Solidarity in decision making tells your relatives that you
agree with your husband. Speaking well of his job and
his employers and coworkers reflects well on your husband also. Handling your finances wisely demonstrates

your husband's ability to provide for you, and it speaks volumes about your trust in him.

In general, negativity breeds negativity, so if you speak against your husband to your extended family, that will be their perception of him. If, for instance, you have a minor spat one day, and you decide to commiserate with your sister or your mom or your cousin. The disagreement with your husband was trivial and short-lasting, but you have given your relative a long-lasting and skewed picture of your husband. Instead, treat him like he's the best husband in the world, and they will come to see the wisdom you demonstrated in marrying such a wonderful, capable man.

worth thinking about

▶ **There are bound** to be some things your extended family and your husband will not agree on. Never go against him in public to side with them.

▶ **It is best** if you do not go to your extended family for financial help because this may only perpetuate any negative feelings they already had about your husband's ability to provide for you. Keep your finances separate as much as possible.

▶ **Your attitude** will be the key indicator of your support for your husband. If others hear you say good things about him, they will tend to have a better attitude toward him.

> *A man shall leave his father and mother and shall be joined to his wife, and the two shall become one flesh.*
> Ephesians 5:31, NAS

question

▼

Why can't you spend every Christmas with your family?

Christmas and other major holidays usually center around traditions and memories. Those who were not part of these original memories can often feel like outsiders looking in. No matter how much your husband loves your parents and siblings, when you got married you became a new family. This doesn't mean you abandon your parents; it just means you are to form your own traditions and create a new history that begins with your husband and extends to your own children.

answer

▼

You probably think your parents and siblings are the best family in the world. You have the neatest family traditions, and you are comfortable with these people who probably know you better than anyone else. However, Christmas is one season best spent with your immediate family as the focus. Insisting on spending every Christmas with your parents may stifle the establishment of these new traditions that are part of the heritage you and your husband pass on to your children.

You can avoid the dilemma of where to spend Christmas right from the beginning by establishing Christmas as belonging to you, your husband, and your children. Share the other holidays, such as Thanksgiving and New Year's Day, with your parents and your husband's parents.

Choosing where to spend Christmas might cause bad feelings, so broach the subject carefully. If you have already been caught in the quandary of always spending Christmas at his or your parents' home, it won't get any easier by putting it off. In this situation, let everyone know early enough that you are going to spend Christmas at home this year, and don't allow guilt to change your plan at the last minute. Your marriage is the most important thing in your life, and sometimes you will need to take a stand to prove that to yourself, to your husband, and to others.

worth thinking about

▶ **Arrange to have** your parents or your husband's parents come to you, if you can accommodate them. If travel is difficult or the distance is great, arrange to have someone accompany them.

▶ **Arrange a family** reunion at a less busy time of the year, or even a joint vacation where all the amenities are provided, such as a cruise or a stay at an all-inclusive resort.

▶ **So that no one** feels left out at the holidays, send a video or current photos of your family to your parents and your husband's parents to help them feel connected to you through this time.

> *This is a time to celebrate before the LORD your God at the designated place of worship he will choose for his name to be honored.*
> Deuteronomy 16:11, NLT

question

Why can't he just accept your family the way they are?

There is a saying that family are friends you don't get to choose. This is especially true in the case of in-laws. You are probably accustomed to how your family acts, and while you may not agree with everything they do, you don't believe they will change. Your husband, however, doesn't have this same relationship with your family. His background may be completely different from yours, and so your family behaviors may be alien to him.

answer

Your husband may have been taught as a child to avoid the exact behaviors that are normal in your family. Perhaps he sees changes in your behavior when you are with your family that he doesn't like. Habits that he has worked hard to overcome may still prevail in your family, and he may feel he is being tempted to return to those habits.

If you sense that your husband distances himself from your family, discourages you from spending time with them, or openly tries to make changes in their behavior, talk with him about his underlying concerns. Address each issue individually. What is it that causes his attitude? Is someone indulging in a behavior he finds unacceptable or uncomfortable to be around? Excessive drinking, tasteless jokes, or other crude behavior? If the behavior relates to some change your husband has made in his own life, he may be willing to offer encouragement to other family members who have expressed an interest in making a change.

While your extended family is important to you, your husband, and your children, they are not your main focus. Consider the example you and your husband are setting for your children, and encourage them to choose wisely and avoid peer pressure. The example you set for your children may be the example your extended family sees that will encourage them to make changes.

worth thinking about

▶ **People will not** generally change their behavior for someone else—they must want to do it for themselves.

▶ **When you get together** with your extended family, arrange activities that are in line with the example you have set for your children.

▶ **Speak privately** with your extended family about behavior that is acceptable in your home and your expectation that they will adhere to that.

> *Don't copy the behavior and customs of this world, but let God transform you into a new person by changing the way you think.*
> Romans 12:2, NLT

question

Why doesn't he see the tension between his family and you?

Very often family dynamics are such that what one person sees as tension, another will see as normal. Large families are perceived as loud and overwhelming to someone from a small family, and small families may seem cold and unemotional to someone who is used to lots of talk and many opinions. What you perceive as tension may not be how your husband sees your interaction with his family.

answer

Your husband knows his family better than you do, and so he understands the nuances in their words and actions. While their behavior may irritate you, he may see it as their normal way of expressing themselves. Unfortunately, once you have concluded that his family doesn't like you for some reason, you may tend to carry that attitude with you and may in fact cause it to be self-perpetuating, as your attitude causes them to treat you differently.

You can alleviate this situation by talking to your husband about your perceptions of his family's attitude toward you. Try to keep the discussion centered on the situation, not the people involved, so that he doesn't feel he or his family is under attack. Limit your comments to specific examples and avoid generalizations about their behavior. Your husband may be able to clarify any misconceptions.

Allow your husband time to consider how he wants to handle the situation. Any decision to cut off contact with a member of his family because of an unwillingness to change should be made with you and your husband in agreement.

Family is important to your marriage, even though you are now your own new family. Being a separate family with your husband and children does not mean you abandon your family or your husband's family. It does mean that you are to put your marriage and family first in your lives.

worth thinking about

▶ **Marriage requires** a change of allegiance from your parents to your spouse. Talking with your husband calmly and rationally will enable you to create an action plan to resolve any tensions that may exist.

▶ **One of the best** things you can do for your family is to teach them the principle that your marriage is the center of your family.

▶ **There is a difference** between tension and feeling uncomfortable with someone. Tension is caused by unresolved conflict, while feeling uncomfortable may be resolved once you get to know the other person. Making the effort to be friendlier can make all the difference.

A gentle answer will calm a person's anger, but an unkind answer will cause more anger.
Proverbs 15:1, NCV

question

How can you question him without undermining his manhood?

answer

I thank You and praise You, O God of my fathers; You have given me wisdom and might, and have now made known to me what we asked of You.

Daniel 2:23, NKJV

question

How can you be supportive of his friendships?

Your husband needs to have friendships with men where he can relax and enjoy their companionship and perhaps even partake in some recreation that you have no interest in. Their time spent together reinforces their masculinity, and in some cases, good friends can become mentors for each other. You can help by allowing your husband the time and energy he needs to develop and maintain these friendships.

answer

With today's hectic lifestyles, it can seem as if encouraging your husband to spend even more time away from you than he already invests in his job goes against the whole idea of family time. However, the time he spends with his friends will invigorate him and allow him some insight into situations other men are going through that may someday be helpful to his own marriage.

The key to successfully supporting his friendships is to discuss how much time he wants to spend with his friends, and then compare that with how much time is realistically available. In looking at your week, decide if you can spend time with your friends at the same time he is out with the guys.

You can encourage guy time by suggesting your husband invite his friends over to your home for a particular sporting event they may want to watch on television. Talk to the other wives and decide if you can rotate this hosting responsibility. Spend time together as couples.

Much of your reluctance to encourage your husband to spend more time with his friends probably exists because you don't want him to get so wrapped up with them that he forgets about you and doesn't spend enough time with you. You can relax. He is married to you, he loves you, and nothing else is as important to him as you are.

worth thinking about

- ▶ When your husband wants to go on a weekend trip with his friends for a tournament or outdoor activity such as hunting or fishing, arrange to go visit family or friends over the same weekend.

- ▶ Just as you seek balance between work and recreation, seek balance among guy time, family time, and couple time for just the two of you.

- ▶ For appearance's sake, any time your husband's friends gather at your home, invite another woman over to help you with snacks.

Friends come and friends go, but a true friend sticks by you like family.
Proverbs 18:24, THE MESSAGE

question

Should you be jealous of his time with his buddies?

Your husband needs to spend time developing relationships with male friends. He needs the support and friendship of other men, and he needs to feel valued in relationships outside your marriage and your family. As a result, you should encourage him to spend time with his buddies. You already know that your marriage and family are the most important relationships your husband has, and you do not need to be jealous of his friends or the time he spends with them.

answer

Time spent in the company of other men will enhance your husband's self-esteem and encourage him in his marriage and family, which should diminish any potential for jealousy you might tend to feel about time spent apart from you. It is only natural to want to spend as much time with your husband as possible, yet it is not necessary to spend all your time together.

One way to overcome feelings of jealousy you might have toward time spent with his friends is to ensure that the time you and your husband spend together enhances your marriage and deepens your relationship. If he wants to spend more time with his friends than he does with you, you need to sit down together and discuss your concerns with him.

Ask him why he likes to spend time with his friends. Time with you should be at least as fulfilling as time with his buddies.

Generally speaking, jealousy arises from some feeling of inadequacy. Knowing you are the most important person in your husband's life will alleviate any doubts you might have, and treating him as the most important person in your life will encourage him to want to spend more time with you.

worth thinking about

▶ **Knowing what** your husband's interests are will ensure that your time together is enjoyable and fulfilling to him. If you aren't sure that's the case, ask him.

▶ **Arrange time** with your girlfriends when your husband spends time with his buddies. If he has a regular time scheduled, consider perhaps taking a class or joining a club.

▶ **Consider the kinds** of things your husband does with his friends, and find a way to include yourself and his friends' wives when appropriate. If all his friends are single, suggest he foster some friendships with married men so you and the other wives can be included from time to time.

Two people are better than one, because they get more done by working together. If one falls down, the other can help him up.
Ecclesiastes 4:9–10, NCV

question

Why doesn't he understand your need for several girlfriends?

While most men have several males in their lives that they would call friends, they tend to have only one or two very close friends at any given time. Women, however, tend to have a cluster of females they would call best friends who actually meet their different emotional needs. Your husband doesn't understand your need for more than one or two close friendships because he doesn't see that need in his own life.

answer

Your husband needs the time he spends with other men and couples you both socialize with. Spending time with his male friends allows him to unwind, to get feedback from other married men, and to develop mentoring relationships.

In some cases, your husband might be jealous of the amount of time and energy you spend with your girlfriends. Talk to him about his feelings and about how each of your friendships benefits you. Discuss his thoughts on the amount of time you spend with each friend. Because spending time with friends should energize you, it will be natural for your husband to be concerned if you are emotionally drained after spending time with one particular friend.

Before deciding to take on any new friends, consider how much more time will be needed to develop and maintain the relationship. Don't be afraid to let a close relationship relax from girlfriend status to friendship. Decide if double-dating as couples can meet your husband's friendship needs as well as yours. Your best friend should be your husband. Your first concern should be your husband. If he sees that he is your best friend and that his emotional needs are being met, he will be more supportive of your other close relationships.

worth thinking about

▶ Relationships are very important to you and to your husband. You will tend to develop and maintain friendships that support you and make you feel good about yourself.

▶ Friendships should never detract from your marriage, even though an emergency may come up from time to time where you will need to take time from your family to spend with a friend. Limit that as much as possible, always explaining to your husband the benefit and the need.

▶ Good friends are hard to find and harder to keep. Be your husband's best friend.

A friend is always loyal, and a brother is born to help in time of need.
Proverbs 17:17, NLT

question

How do you deal with celebrations that include an ex-spouse?

With the high incidence of divorce in America today, at some point in your marriage you might need to deal with an ex-husband or ex-wife at a family gathering. Knowing in advance that in most cases people will behave themselves in large groups may set your mind at ease. Also, remembering that this time is about family and not your differences will help you and your husband cope with the situation.

answer

Regardless of whether the ex is yours or his, the ex's presence can cause many old feelings to surface. It can be easy to bury unresolved issues under the everyday life you now live, but more difficult to do so when the subject of those feelings is sitting across the room from you. Discuss with your husband how you will deal with the ex's presence at weddings, funerals, graduations, holidays such as Christmas and Thanksgiving, and family reunions.

First and foremost, you must both make the determination that the family gathering is not about your feelings or about who was right or wrong in the breakup. The family gathering is about family, and although you may all be related, you don't all feel the same way about the ex. Determine to be cordial and not make a scene no matter what happens or what remarks drift your way.

If possible, minimize the length of time you are in close proximity to the ex. Arrange to have a neutral party accompany you so that if you accidentally run into the ex, you will be more likely to stay calm. If you think that it will be absolutely impossible for you to stay cool at the gathering, you may be able to arrange an alternate smaller group before or after the main event For example, you might host a breakfast for a smaller circle of guests that doesn't include the ex prior to a wedding.

worth thinking about

▶ Talk to your husband about any concerns he may have about an ex being present at your next upcoming event. Make plans about how to avoid confrontation. You may want to role-play the situation so you both have some ideas on what might come up.

▶ Regardless of how many people agree with you about the ex, be willing to set the example of good behavior and hospitality.

▶ Oftentimes, making the first move of cordiality will catch the ex off guard. Smile, shake hands, and compliment the ex's looks. Then move on to another group of people.

An angry man stirs up strife, and a furious man abounds in transgression.
Proverbs 29:22, NKJV

80

question
▼
Why are joint bank accounts a good idea?

When you and your husband got married, you pledged yourselves to each other for the rest of your lives. You each decided that you are better together than apart, and this same truth holds for all of your assets, including bank accounts. Joint bank accounts are a good idea because of what they say about your marriage: you trust each other, and you do not have any secrets from each other.

answer
▼

Joint bank accounts show love by making sure that your bank accounts are available to either one of you in the case of emergency. This simple form of preplanning shows care and concern for your husband as you take steps to bring every area of your life into unity with him. At a time when you are already faced with overwhelming and often difficult decisions, finances should not be an issue.

Combining your funds makes the money go farther as you share in expenses, and having your money in one account helps in the budgeting process because a shortfall in income is more easily absorbed. Your record keeping is simpler, and with both of you contributing to the account, there is an aspect of accountability for your spending. Even if there is only one income earner in your household, having joint bank accounts means that either you or he can pay bills and shop for the family. The perception of ownership of the money is removed, enabling you both to feel ownership in your family finances.

Overall, couples who have joint bank accounts tend to agree more over their finances, make more financial decisions together, and are in a better position financially than couples who keep their accounts separate. Unity in marriage is important, and often that unity is demonstrated in your trust for each other where money is concerned.

worth thinking about

▶ **To make sure** you know where you stand with your accounts and bills, it is best if one person makes sure the bills are paid each month. Share the burden by having the other person balance the checkbook.

▶ **Joint accounts** are not limited to checking accounts. Joint assets are a good idea for all the same reasons as are joint accounts.

▶ **Separate accounts** are good if you like to plan special surprises for each other that take more than pocket cash, such as anniversaries, vacations, or larger gifts. Decide together how much money will be put in the separate accounts each month.

> *Her husband trusts her without reserve, and never has reason to regret it.*
> Proverbs 31:11, THE MESSAGE

question

When is it okay to take separate vacations?

Joint vacations for married couples are a time of shared experiences, a respite away from jobs and other obligations, and an opportunity to spend time with the one you love. However, some circumstances might require you to take separate vacations, such as your husband not being able to take time off, your accompanying other female relatives or visiting family, or your husband not knowing anyone at your high school or college reunion. Separate vacations should be limited, and you should make every attempt to spend your leisure time together.

answer

There are people who find it difficult to take time off, and your husband may be one of those people. Encourage your husband to mentor someone at work who can help him out on a regular basis and who can fill in for him during vacations. Schedule your vacations around his least busy times of the year if possible. If your husband struggles with leaving his job for a week or more at a time, arrange several minivacations throughout the year where you can take a three- or four-day weekend and get away together.

If you have more vacation time than your husband, consider volunteering at a local community event, taking a class such as painting, or engaging in another activity you'd like to pursue. Arrange your time so that when your husband is home for the evening or weekend, you are free to spend time with him.

Spending time together as a couple and as a family is important. Leisure time gives you the opportunity to relax and open up with each other away from the distractions and problems of everyday life. Encourage your husband to spend more time with you by letting him know he is special to you.

worth thinking about

▶ **If your husband** really doesn't want to go to your high school reunion, don't force the issue. Consider cutting the trip short by a couple of days and going home early.

▶ **If you choose** to go on vacation without your husband, traveling with a women's group or church friends can provide companionship and a variety of interests to choose from.

▶ **Encourage your husband** to go on vacation with you by choosing a destination and activities you are both interested in.

> *The way God designed our bodies is a model for understanding our lives together as a church: every part dependent on every other part, the parts we mention and the parts we don't, the parts we see and the parts we don't.*
>
> 1 Corinthians 12:25, THE MESSAGE

question

▼

How much of your past does he need to know?

Sharing details of your past creates vulnerability and depends on trust to not create a division between people. Sometimes knowing too much about a person's past changes the way you think of him or treat him. When it comes to your marriage, it is important to be able to create an atmosphere of trust and openness. Your life experiences have made you the person you are today, and in some cases, for your husband to really understand you, he may need to know some details of your past.

answer

▼

Your husband needs to know anything in your past that might affect him directly or that could be used against either of you in the future. Because your marriage is a combining of two people, everything that belonged to one now becomes part of the other person. You should tell your husband your medical history in case of an emergency where you are unable to speak for yourself. Include any pertinent family health information such as hereditary or genetic issues.

Your husband doesn't need to know names or details of past relationships you may have had, because those relationships no longer exist. He does need to know that his past is safe with you, and you can encourage him to talk about his prior relationships when he feels comfortable.

While your current condition and/or situation may be a product of choices you made in the past, any bad choices that you made don't necessarily reflect badly on you. In fact, as your husband learns that you are not that same person anymore, and that you have learned from those bad choices, he will actually trust you more.

worth thinking about

- ▶ If your husband finds out about your past from someone else, he might tend to trust you less, because he may see the fact that you withheld this from him as a sign you don't trust him with the information.

- ▶ When you make the decision to share your past with him, it isn't necessary to reveal it all at once. You can break it into smaller sections if need be, such as past relationships, habits you have changed, or choices you made.

- ▶ It should be easy to share the good memories of the past with your husband. Pull out the photo albums or old family movies, make a bowl of popcorn, and laugh at yourself.

> *I will put aside my anger and*
> *forget the evil of earlier days.*
> Isaiah 65:16, NLT

83

question

▼

How and when do you tell him he has bad breath?

No matter how good your oral hygiene is, there are circumstances where you may end up with an odor on your breath. Bad breath can be caused by indigestion, food, beverages, smoking, or an infection. Your husband may not know that he has bad breath. You should tell him privately as soon as you notice it, and have a remedy for the situation, at least in the short term.

answer

▼

Begin by asking him if he thinks your breath needs to be freshened. Then offer to check his breath for him. If you decide that his breath is stale, let him know. Having a breath mint or gum on hand will offer an immediate solution.

Try to determine what causes the bad odor. While most people understand that spicy food—as well as coffee or smoking—can be a culprit, many people don't know that a tooth infection or a digestive problem may be the cause. If necessary, visit your dentist to rule out tooth decay and infection.

Many times bad breath creates an impression on others that the sufferer doesn't care if he is being offensive, and the perception of poor hygiene may reflect badly on your husband. If you notice others avoiding close contact with him during conversation, let your husband know that it isn't just your opinion that matters. In most cases, he will be more than willing to take steps not to offend others.

In business relationships as well as with family and friends, it is sometimes necessary to work in close contact with other people. Your husband is most likely diligent about other aspects of his personal hygiene, and oral hygiene should be no exception. When you and your husband take a proactive approach to your public contact with others, you can help each other by being diligent in noticing what the other needs.

worth thinking about

▶ **Develop a secret** word or symbol with which you can let each other know when refreshing is needed.

▶ **Choosing to limit** coffee and spicy food unless you are able to brush your teeth or use a mouth rinse may be a solution.

▶ **Sometimes if a person** is nervous or anxious, he tends to produce less saliva, which causes dry mouth and increases the potential for breath odor. If your husband is going into a situation where he might be nervous, suggest he carry hard candy or take bottled water to drink.

> *I said, "I will climb the palm tree, I will take hold of its fruit stalks." Oh, may your breasts be like clusters of the vine, and the fragrance of your breath like apples.*
> Song of Solomon 7:8, NAS

question

How do you
respond when
he embarrasses you?

No one likes to be embarrassed, and particularly not by someone else. Intentionally embarrassing another person is many times a response to being hurt or wanting to make the other person look bad. In most cases you will probably find that when your husband's words or actions have embarrassed you, it was completely unintentional. You can choose to love your husband despite his behavior by reminding yourself that love is not circumstantial—it is a choice.

answer

If you choose to love your husband only when you feel like it or when he deserves it, you will probably be able to find many reasons not to love him. If, however, you recognize that you choose to love him even if he embarrasses you, then you will be able to look past his behavior and focus on his motives.

Talk to your husband if something he does embarrasses you, especially if it is something that he has done repeatedly. Let him know how it makes you feel when he does it. If you know that others around him are also embarrassed, let him know. Suggest an alternative attitude or behavior for him in a similar situation. Let him know when you see he has attempted to change his behavior.

If you see that others around you are not acting uncomfortable with his behavior, consider whether you might be overreacting. Etiquette and societal expectations can change over time, and perhaps you are being overly sensitive.

If your husband seems to be embarrassing you as a response to your behavior, consider whether something you said or did offended him in some way. If so, apologize to him, even if it was inadvertent, and then discuss alternative ways to handle your reactions in the future.

worth thinking about

▶ **Any discussions** you have about what you consider to be embarrassing behavior should be done in private.

▶ **Even if the behavior** is completely inadvertent, such as excessive flatulence, consider changes you might make. For example, flatulence can be caused by eating too much, or it might be what was consumed. While common culprits are legumes or green leafy vegetables, sometimes tomato products and citrus juices can cause the same symptoms if one takes in too much of a certain food or drink.

▶ **Choosing to love** him is not a decision you make once and it is done. Sometimes you may need to make that choice several times a day.

> *God blesses those who do not turn away because of me.*
> Matthew 11:6, NLT

question

How do you handle not knowing where your husband is?

Wanting to be with your husband and to spend time with him is a natural outflow of a good marriage. The secret to being able to allow your husband the freedom he needs to live a productive and independent life while still being accountable for his actions is to let him know that your concerns are based not in mistrust or fatalism but in his well-being and safety.

answer

There could be any number of reasons why you may not know where your husband is at any given point of time. He should not feel that he needs to let you know if he is going to be slightly later than expected. Everyday circumstances such as traffic, workload, or inattention to time can delay his arrival. Discuss with him what the maximum delay factor is for both of you before you will be expected to make a phone call.

There are specific situations where his failure to be accounted for could indicate a problem. These might include driving alone at night, traveling in bad weather, or meeting in an unfamiliar place. Before he does any of these things, discuss contingency plans for keeping in touch and how he will let you know if he needs help.

When he travels, it is fine to know where he is going and when he expects to get there. Allow some range of movement in his itinerary, and decide whom you will call if he doesn't arrive.

Being concerned when he isn't where he said he would be can be a product of needless worry. Consider if you are trying to control him too much. It is not necessary to know where he is every minute. It is fine to let him know that you worry when you aren't kept in the know, but you can also assure him that you trust him and you are not just checking up on him.

worth thinking about

▶ **If you struggle** with not knowing where your husband is, it could be because of a lack of trust. If so, talk to your husband about ways you can keep in touch more, such as by cell phone. Many times just knowing you can call will be enough to allay your concerns.

▶ **If there are** potential emergency issues—such as medical problems—that might require your being able to get ahold of your husband quickly, consider a pager. Many times these work in areas where a cell phone won't.

▶ **If you worry** more when your husband travels, pray together before he leaves. Keep in touch daily while he is gone.

> *I pray that the God who gives hope will fill you with much joy and peace while you trust in him.*
> Romans 15:13, NCV

question

How do you encourage him in his relationship with God?

answer

Grow in the grace and knowledge of our Lord and Savior Jesus Christ.

2 Peter 3:18, NIV

question

What's the best way to fit couple time into your busy schedule?

There are many things that fill your schedule, including jobs, family, hobbies, looking after your home, shopping, and preparing meals. It seems there aren't enough hours in the day to get everything done. What happens too often is that time for you as a couple is neglected because everything and everyone else has priority. If you don't make a point of scheduling couple time, it won't happen on its own.

answer

Many times couples find they have packed their schedules so full of other commitments that they haven't left time for them, as a couple. This can happen when you feel that your marriage is solid and secure and doesn't need any pampering. It can also happen when some other area of your life seems needier than your marriage. Jobs, children, and everyday living activities can take up the majority of your time.

Instead of trying to add time together to your list, look for something you can take off your list and then replace it with your couple time. Do things where you can talk with each other instead of things where you are required to listen to something or someone else.

Choose activities you both like to do, and do them together. Shared pastimes create a bond of trust that strengthens your marriage. Both of you could decide to give up something you would have done separately to allow a shared time together.

Full calendars and packed schedules don't translate into a fulfilling marriage. Focus on each other and your marriage relationship, and the benefits will overflow into all areas of your lives. The key to finding time for you as a couple is to want to do it. There will always be reasons not to look for a good excuse to spend more time together.

worth thinking about

▶ Exhaustion can steal your enthusiasm for enjoying time together. Go to bed early one night a week, and talk until you fall asleep.

▶ The good news is that couple time doesn't have to be just another thing to do. Look forward to spending time with the love of your life, and it will become a joy, not a chore.

▶ During couple time, you should be able to talk if you want to, or not. Look for ways to spend time alone together.

We took sweet counsel together, and walked to the house of God in the throng.
Psalm 55:14, NKJV

question

What if you need to be alone?

There are many reasons to want to spend time by your-self, including feeling overwhelmed or having a need to work out some issue you are facing. However, if your husband perceives that being alone is not the answer, he may try to intrude on that solitude. Getting refreshed allows you to give more time and energy to your husband when you are with him. Establishing guidelines so that both of you know when being alone is best for you is key to letting him know that this will be good.

answer

Spending time alone appears to go against one of the reasons why you got married in the first place, which was to spend time together. In your busy lives, time together is already at a premium, and so your husband may not like the idea of your spending any more time apart than necessary. Be sure you spend some quality time together every day, even if it's just a few minutes.

Because the energy you expend on relationship building can be draining, you need a mechanism for restoration. Sometimes the emotional exhaustion is so pervasive that you may not be able to properly voice your desire. There are many biblical examples of people who spent time alone for direction and restoration, including David, Moses, and Jesus.

Communication is the key to understanding. Explaining to your husband that you simply need time to recharge will set the stage for his being accepting of your time alone. Your time alone should be spent in activities that refresh and renew your mind, spirit, and body.

Many times you will receive insights and solutions to situations and problems that have eluded you, and you will be able to share that with your husband. This doesn't mean you don't want his input, because you do. Let him know you appreciate his concern, and reinforce your love for him by spending extra quality time with him before and after your alone time.

worth thinking about

▶ If your husband sees that the time you spend alone produces the desired results, he will be much more likely to encourage your solitude in the future.

▶ Do not use this alone time as punishment for disagreements. Your alone time should always be positive, even if you are working through a problem.

▶ Not everyone needs the same amount of alone time. Try to structure your time during periods when your husband is occupied with something else.

> *Bring me back that I may be restored,*
> *for You are the LORD my God.*
> Jeremiah 31:18, NAS

question

▼

How can you create a special dinner for him?

When envisioning romance and love, a darkened restaurant and a table adorned with linen, crystal, and fine china often come to mind. Perhaps you have a special memory of a dinner date that included a candle on the table and soft music in the background. There is something about the flickering of a candle that speaks of intimacy, special times together, and holding hands across the table. Surprising your husband with a candlelight dinner will remind him not only of those times together, but also of why he fell in love with you to begin with.

answer

▼

Even if you and your husband never went to such a fancy restaurant before you were married, you can still create this romantic getaway in your own home. Candlelight and other soft lighting cover a multitude of deficiencies, so even if you don't have fine linen and crystal and your wine is simply grape juice in a water goblet, romance will still be in the air.

The extra effort you put into having a candlelight dinner for him might surprise him. If he asks what the special occasion is, make sure he understands that the dinner is because he deserves it. Have a nice meal ready, perhaps a light dessert for afterward, and the setting is ready for romance.

Your extra efforts might even encourage your husband to return the favor at some point in the future and surprise you with a special dinner. The important thing, though, is not to attach strings to this time together. You are doing this because you love him and because you want to show him in a tangible way that you desire him and still think he's the sexiest man you've ever met.

Having a candlelight dinner just for two will remind both of you that your marriage is important to you, that personal intimate times create closeness between you, and that you are important to each other.

worth thinking about

▶ **If you have children**, think about sending them to a friend's house for a sleepover. Maybe trade evenings with a friend so you can do this more often; you can return the favor by letting them have their own romantic evenings while you watch their kids.

▶ **Soft music** in the background helps set the stage, and it also fills in those quiet moments when you are gazing into each other's eyes.

▶ **Candlelight is always** kind to the eye, softening wrinkles and bringing a sparkle to your eyes.

> *You will see and be radiant,*
> *and your heart will thrill and rejoice.*
> Isaiah 60:5, NAS

question

Why does he treat you differently now that you're married?

When you and your husband were dating, you both were probably on your best behavior, each wanting to impress the other with your witty charm, good manners, and intelligent talk. Regardless of how long you dated or how long your engagement was, you didn't know the real person. Since you married, you both have probably felt comfortable enough with each other that the niceties of courtship are no longer needed, and now you can be your real selves around each other.

answer

While changes in attitude may be a fact, it is never too late to make changes in your behavior to show just how much you mean to each other. Marriage should never be an excuse to take each other for granted. Your marriage license is not written permission to treat each other badly. While dating can be like a game, it is hard to keep up the charade for the long term. The fact is that marriage should be a reason to treat each other better, not worse, as you get to know each other better, spend more time together, and invest in each other and your marriage.

Regardless of how you think your husband is treating you now since you are married, you can set the example by treating him like the prince he is. Take time to tell him often how much you love him. Make time to spend together, even if it's just sitting in front of a fire or taking a walk around the block.

Consider your own attitude toward your husband to see if you might be sending him hidden messages that you are taking him for granted. By making changes in your own attitude first, you will be more likely to see changes in him. Share your concerns with him, and talk about ways you can show each other how much you mean to each other.

worth thinking about

▶ **Mark at least** one night a month on your calendar as a date night. Alternate which of you will be responsible for such details as where you go and what you do. You don't have to spend a lot of money. Even a visit to the local ice-cream parlor can bring back good memories of your courtship.

▶ **Leave a love note** in his shaving bag, especially if he is going out of town.

▶ **Make a list** of all the ways he shows you he loves you, and keep it somewhere safe where you can find it when you start to feel as if you are being taken for granted again.

> *Make my joy complete by being of the same mind, maintaining the same love, united in spirit, intent on one purpose.*
>
> Philippians 2:2, NAS

question

▼

How do you show that you love being married to him?

You might think that your husband knows you love being married to him because you choose to stay with him, you tell him you love him, or you take care of the kids and the house. In fact, anyone can fulfill those roles; the role of his wife and lover and best friend is a role no one else can fill except you. Show your husband you love being married to him by protecting your marriage from attack and by standing strong in your commitment to him and to your family.

answer

▼

Families and marriages are very much under attack in society today, from both the inside and the outside. Inside attacks include infidelity, pornography, inattention, and complacency. Outside attacks include societal attitudes regarding the sanctity and definition of marriage, as well as job pressures and financial strains.

You can show your husband that you are committed to your marriage by placing hedges of protection around your marriage and the behavior of the people in your household. Demonstrate your solidarity with his ability to lead and protect your family through agreement and calm discussion. Set the example for your children that marriage and family are important by making sure they see that you place your marriage and family above anything else in your lives.

When you love someone, you want to do what is best for that person. The same is true of your marriage. Your marriage is an outward representation of your love for and commitment to your husband, your desire to work through the problems that life throws at you, and your recognition that you are stronger together than you are individually. Your children benefit from a solid marriage relationship through that stability, and they will be more likely to have strong, lasting marriages themselves, which is good for the next generation coming along.

worth thinking about

▶ **Tell your husband** all the good things you are thankful for that have come from your marriage. Don't limit the list to the material things—include changes you have seen in him and in you.

▶ **Honor your husband** with your actions as well as your words. Treat him with respect around others and when you are alone.

▶ **Teach your children** to demonstrate their love and respect for their father, and have them tell their dad how glad they are he is their father.

> *Whoever tries to live right and be loyal finds life, success, and honor.*
> Proverbs 21:21, NCV

91

question

How do you know he really wants your relationship to succeed?

With the divorce rate standing at more than 50 percent, it might be easy to think that many people view marriage as less than permanent. Studies have shown that when people consider divorce an option, the marriage tends not to persevere. You can know if your husband really wants your marriage to last by listening to his words, knowing his heart, and understanding how he demonstrates faithfulness and commitment.

answer

It is easy to believe your husband loves you and enjoys your marriage when things are going well. However, when you are struggling in some way, his words may tell you more about his feelings. Listen carefully to what he says. If he never uses the word *divorce* as a threat or an option, you can be assured he is most likely committed to the success and longevity of your marriage.

You can know what your husband is feeling about your relationship by his response to attacks on it. If you see he is hurt when you disagree on an issue, you can know that he wants unity. If he defends you to others and praises you sincerely, this is a sign of his devotion.

Your husband will likely demonstrate his faithfulness and commitment to you and your marriage in several ways. Needless to say, sexual and relational fidelity is important to showing his desire for your marriage to succeed. He will make changes as appropriate, and he will listen to your concerns, allow your input into decisions, and validate your feelings.

In short, your husband will show you in all areas of his life and relationship with you that he not only wants your relationship to succeed, but he also wants it to grow and improve.

worth thinking about

▶ **Being committed** to your marriage doesn't only mean he comes home every night for dinner. It also means that he values your marriage relationship above all other relationships and puts its well-being ahead of anything else in his life.

▶ **You can show** your husband that you appreciate the time and energy he invests in your marriage by making sure your relationship with him is more important than any other relationship.

▶ **When divorce** is not an option, love, perseverance, respect, and honor will fill in the gaps. Don't use the word *divorce* as a weapon, and don't keep it as plan B.

> *If they listen and obey God, they will be blessed with prosperity throughout their lives. All their years will be pleasant.*
> Job 36:11, NLT

question

How do random acts of kindness enhance your love?

You can add some variety to your expressions of affection by using random acts of kindness—doing something nice just because. Random acts enhance your expressions of love by letting your husband know that you were thinking of him perhaps at the most unlikely time, and that your feelings of connection go far beyond your physical togetherness.

answer

It can be easy to fall into a pattern of how you express your feelings, such as with hugs, kisses, or words. Random acts of kindness are wonderful because they are not connected with a special occasion such as a birthday or an anniversary. The complete unexpectedness of these acts will surprise and delight your husband.

You can look for ways to please him in your everyday activities, particularly if you can find a way to help him accomplish some of his goals. Any time you can reduce his workload and free up his time, you will enable him to feel more productive and will reduce his stress.

Other ways that random acts of kindness will please your husband and enhance your connection include partnering with him on a project that you wouldn't normally take part in. Your desire to spend time with your husband and give up your time to do something out of your norm makes the gift even more valuable.

Random acts of kindness can also be done for your husband without his knowing who did them. If you have children, encourage them to participate in these random acts without claiming ownership. The entire family will learn that giving to others is a special gift in itself.

worth thinking about

▶ **Listen to your husband** as he tells you some of his dreams and goals. You can probably find several ways to help him achieve those dreams and goals.

▶ **Regardless of how** you and your husband have divided the household chores, your husband will be delighted if you do something he was supposed to do. It doesn't have to be every time—even just once will please him.

▶ **Encourage random acts** of kindness for each other by not attaching any strings to them, such as for a special occasion or because you knew he was tired or busy.

> *Show your kindness to me, your servant.*
> *Save me because of your love.*
> Psalm 31:16, NCV

question

▼

How can love feel like a gift instead of an obligation?

Love and marriage are two of the greatest gifts that God created for people to enjoy. Being in love and feeling loved can strengthen you to withstand the many storms of life. Over time, however, it may feel like you are just going through the motions. While the commitment is still strong, the feelings associated with it may have dulled. You can keep love feeling like a gift—one you give and receive daily—by taking steps to keep it fresh and alive every day.

answer

▼

Marriage and love can draw you and your husband together in a bond that is not meant to be broken. You can think of marriage as being like the contents of your refrigerator. If you do your grocery shopping once a year and stock up on all the food you are going to eat in that year, after a couple of months, the food will be stale and unappetizing.

Marriage can be the same every day unless you make a point of bringing fresh thoughts and emotions into your marriage on a daily basis. You can start with choosing to show your love in a new way. Begin each day with hugs and kisses, and send him off to work with a word of encouragement. If your intimate life has fallen into a routine of when and where, make a change.

Another way to keep your marriage alive and fresh is not to depend on your feelings to determine how and when to express your love. Decide that no matter how stressed you may feel, you will greet your husband with a special dinner when he comes home tonight. Arrange a surprise date night out, or rent a movie on the spur of the moment you know he will enjoy.

When you make the decision to put aside your own feelings and needs, your husband will recognize this gift you are giving. Just as God shows His love to you in different ways each day, consider how you can show your love to your husband today.

worth thinking about

▶ **The main difference** between a gift and an obligation is in the attitude of the giver. When you do something nice for your husband because he deserves it, it will feel like a gift.

▶ **When you** and your husband truly seek to please each other and express your love, the thoughts associated with doing so are what is important.

▶ **God gave His Son** before you ever knew Him or acknowledged the gift. When you give a gift with love as its motive, at some point your husband will see it and thank you for it.

Relish life with the spouse you love each and every day.
Ecclesiastes 9:9, THE MESSAGE

question

How can you protect your marriage?

Many people think that once they are married, their worries are over. They have the piece of paper that says they belong with their spouse. However, a marriage is a living, growing thing, and it must be nurtured, nourished, and protected just like any other living thing. You protect your marriage through prayer, time spent together, common goals, and already having made decisions in advance regarding how to deal with specific situations that will come up in the course of your marriage.

answer

Your wedding vows laid the groundwork for your intentions for your marriage. While your vows are important, they are really just a starting place for the protection of your marriage. Your vows address the what, but not the how, of ensuring the success of your relationship.

The most important way to protect your marriage is through prayer. Studies have shown that couples who pray together experience a lower rate of separation and divorce. Daily prayer is recommended, and you can start this new habit at any time. Praying for and about your marriage is key, as well as praying for protection from temptation for each of you.

Your attitude toward your marriage will ensure it is strong and protected. When you don't take your marriage for granted, you will invest time and energy into it. Just as with any other living thing, your marriage is not going to sustain itself just because you want it to.

Spending time talking out any issues that come up and applying those discussions to similar situations when they occur will help your marriage flourish. Decisions made in advance can help you when you are faced with a particular situation that you haven't faced before. Standing in unity and knowing your direction will enable you and your marriage to come through the storms of life stronger than ever.

worth thinking about

► If you treat your marriage casually, the result will likely be instability and insecurity. Instead, treat your marriage as the serious and precious gift from God that it is.

► When you and your husband act as if you were always together, not allowing any hint of jealousy or impropriety to sneak into your behavior strengthens your relationship.

► You are pledged to each other and only each other, and need not do or say anything to attract the attention of the opposite sex, including glances, mode of dress, or speech.

> *Guard your heart above all else,*
> *for it determines the course of your life.*
> Proverbs 4:23, NLT

question

▼

Why spark the romance in your marriage?

Feeling good about your marriage can help you feel good about other areas of your life. Romantic feelings about your husband include not only sexual intimacy but also trust, respect, and friendship. Romance in your marriage will increase your interest in each other, and it will tend to cause you to want to spend more time together. Romance also will create stability within your relationship and will help you learn more about how your husband thinks.

answer

▼

Feelings and instances of romance aren't created automatically. You will probably need to put some thought and effort into it. Even a person who is categorized as being a romantic invests time and energy into putting action to ideas.

Creating a romantic setting can increase sexual interest and may lead to a more satisfying intimate time together. While not all romance needs to end in sex, creating and sustaining sexual interest in each other enhances your feelings of connection with each other.

Sparking the romance in your marriage can make you feel special and desirable, which will impact how you view your role in your marriage. As well, when you feel special, your attitude will show, which will tend to increase your husband's interest as well.

Romance is a collection of tools that you can employ in your marriage to increase your emotional connection to your husband. As you increase that connection, you will find that you have created a circle that will encourage your husband in his attention toward you, while giving him a deeper sense of connection and commitment to you and to your marriage.

worth thinking about

▶ **A recent survey** showed that men would like their wives to initiate sex more often. Create a spark of interest by putting the move on your husband.

▶ **Romance is not** just about flowers and candlelight. Any time can be romantic when you create an intimate time for you and your husband.

▶ **If you struggle** to come up with ideas, ask your husband to plan a romantic evening or weekend for both of you. Afterward talk about what really made it special, and use his comments to plan your next romantic getaway.

How beautiful you are and how pleasing,
O love, with your delights!
Song of Solomon 7:6, NIV

Why is he the perfect man for you?

On the basis of faith in His name, it is the name of Jesus which has strengthened this man whom you see and know.

Acts 3:16, NAS

question

How can you help him
feel lovable?

There is a difference between feeling loved and feeling
lovable. Your husband probably already knows that you
love him. Feeling lovable comes from within a person
and is closely related to feelings of self-worth. You can
help your husband know that he is lovable—worthy of
being loved—by helping him see himself as you see
him. You can show him through your attitude and your
encouragement, by allowing him to express his feelings,
and by showing him love in a way he understands.

answer

While many people can express feelings of love, sometimes their own feelings of being worthy of being loved
can get in the way of being able to receive love. When a
person can receive love, he is nourished and nurtured by
that love. However, if he cannot accept that he is loved,
he can become weary and exhausted as he tries to give
something he does not have within him. God made you
to love and be loved, and to desire love from Him and
from others.

You can help your husband understand his worth to you
and to God by having a good attitude. He will feel more

secure and successful in his marriage if he knows that your attitude won't fluctuate toward him.

Understanding how your husband gives and receives love will encourage him as you respond to him. Visible results of his efforts at connecting with you can be very encouraging to him.

When your husband feels worthy of being loved, those feelings will extend to others, including you. Show your husband that he deserves to be loved because of who he is. Although his job or his contribution to his family may change, who your husband is—his values, plans, dreams, and commitment to you—will always remain.

worth thinking about

▶ Encourage your husband in how he shows love, even if it isn't your particular love language. That he shows love is more important than how he does it.

▶ If you see that he struggles with feelings of self-worth, make a list of all the things you love about him. Don't include things he does or doesn't do. Instead, focus on his values and intentions.

▶ It can be hard to help someone else see that he is worthy of love if you don't feel it for yourself. If you struggle in this area, talk to your husband, and pray together that God would show both of you just how much you are loved.

> *You have no idea how good your love makes me feel.*
> Philemon 1:7, THE MESSAGE

97

question

How do you get past your last argument?

Most married couples have disagreements at one time or another. How you resolve conflict sets the tone for the success of your marriage. It doesn't matter who is right or who is wrong in an argument. What matters is how you handle the situation. It is difficult to feel loving toward someone you are angry with. Getting past those feelings will restore your marriage relationship, and you will both grow to a new level of maturity and understanding.

answer

An argument is a lot like an open wound—emotions and fears have been opened up, and unless they are dealt with quickly, infection will set in. The good news is that healing is available, regardless of how big the argument or how angry you are.

After an argument, your initial reaction may be to withdraw from your husband to avoid the conflict. This may make you feel better at first, but not talking about it won't help the situation or prevent it from becoming an argument again in the future. As a couple, you need to look at the cause of the argument. Don't grasp at the first thing that comes to mind, because that isn't usually the true cause. Instead, be willing to dig deeper into the matter.

Many times an argument occurs because of differing expectations. When your expectations are not met, you may feel as if your husband doesn't care. Sometimes the issue may be that he doesn't know what you want. You can bring a quick resolution to your argument by talking calmly about the issues, always seeking a solution.

Open and honest discussion of the cause of the argument will clear the air and will show your husband that you really love him and want to be emotionally and physically close to him. Admitting you were both wrong will show maturity and a willingness to grow closer together.

worth thinking about

▶ **It is difficult** to be angry at your husband when you are praying for him. At the first sign of irritation, stop and pray.

▶ **You and your** husband argue because you hold differing opinions or viewpoints on the particular matter under discussion. Find some common ground and start there.

▶ While "kissing and making up" is a good way to affirm your love, it shouldn't be the only way. If it is, take a look at your conflict resolution skills, and look for other ways to resolve differences.

Everyone who confesses that Jesus is God's Son participates continuously in an intimate relationship with God.
1 John 4:15, THE MESSAGE

question

How do you say you're sorry?

It is nearly impossible to be right all the time—only God can really claim that. As a result, you can be pretty certain that at some point in your marriage you are going to need to apologize to your husband. The good news is that you can say you're sorry and not lose credibility with him if you apologize quickly and with sincerity.

answer

There is no doubt that if you apologize before your error is noticed by someone else, you will tend to be held in higher esteem. This is particularly true if your apology is directed toward your husband. The husband-wife relationship is meant to be one of intimacy and support. If your husband feels as though he has to bring an error to your attention, however, then he may feel like a parent. To avoid this, as soon as you become aware of the mistake, apologize and ask for suggestions on how to avoid it in the future.

While apologies are not the most pleasant thing to give, they can be a most welcome gift to the recipient. In a world where many want to lay blame on someone else, it is refreshing when a person takes responsibility for her actions. Ask your friends and family—they probably know people who have never said they were sorry, and will be remembered for that.

Sincerity in an apology is key to its being accepted and believed. Changes in behavior and attitude will ensure the recipient that you really mean what you say.

Saying you're sorry, particularly to your husband, will go a long way toward mending a relationship that may have been torn. Sometimes a simple "I'm sorry" will help both of you get over the moment, past the hurt feelings, and enable you to focus on the real issue.

worth thinking about

▶ When you know what your husband's love language is, you can apply this to how you apologize. For example, if his love language is time, you can apologize by setting aside time for the two of you to be alone together.

▶ Regardless of how big the disagreement or how late in the day it happened, never go to sleep angry with each other.

▶ When you and your husband disagree about something, it really doesn't matter who is right and who is wrong. Even if you are completely right in your position, being at odds with him is wrong. Apologize for your attitude and ask if you can talk about it again.

> *I'm sorry—forgive me. I'll never do that again, I promise!*
> Job 42:6, THE MESSAGE

What is the best gift you could give your husband?

When you think of the word *gift* you probably envision going shopping, which may or may not be an enjoyable activity for you. The truth is, when considering the best gift you could give your husband, you won't need to go to a store or shop online or order from a catalog. Instead, the best thing you could give your husband is well within your means, regardless of your budget, and will not take anything more than the rest of your life. The best gift you possibly could give your husband is your love.

answer

The best form of love you can give your husband is the kind of love that God gives you—unconditional love that desires the best for you, that puts its needs to one side to ensure your needs are met, and that never does anything to harm you. This type of love—*agape* love—is the same type that Jesus talked about when He said that love is laying down your life for someone else.

When you love your husband with this kind of unconditional love, you will seek to please him. Your words will be carefully weighed before you speak them, and he will be in your thoughts often. *Agape* love means that selfishness is nonexistent because everything you do is to benefit him. It doesn't mean you give him everything he wants or asks for, because that may not always be the best for him or even possible. It simply means that your love is a pure love, one untainted by such negative hindrances as tit-for-tat retaliation or not-very-funny put-downs.

Agape love—the kind of love God shows you—is never diminished in the giving—it is multiplied. *Agape* love grows and matures, finds new ways to delight, will carry you through the tough times, and will draw you and your husband together in a bond of such intimacy and understanding that it cannot be broken.

worth thinking about

▶ *Agape* love never has selfish undertones, but always seeks the best for the other person.

▶ With true *agape* love, there is no mistrust or jealousy. It is patient and kind, and makes others want to be more like you.

▶ Loving your husband may not always be easy or fun, but it will always be right. The only way you can truly love is to spend time in God's presence, getting to know Him better.

> *Every good thing given and every perfect gift is from above, coming down from the Father.*
> James 1:17, NAS

question

Is love just a chemical reaction, or is there something else?

Being in love causes the body to release endorphins that make you feel better, make you healthier, and may even help you live longer. However, love is not just a chemical reaction—it is a decision you make, not just once, but many times. Your decision to love your husband on a daily basis will be based on your overall goals for your marriage, your commitment to each other, and your desire to please God with your faithfulness.

answer

Loving your husband is always easy when things are going well, but more difficult when you are in the midst of struggles. The decision to love will draw you together through the struggle and will enable both you and your husband to grow emotionally and relationally.

Loving your husband is not just an action—it is a decision reinforced by your actions. You may well need to make that decision on a daily basis. He is bound to say or do something that will make you question your decision. Do not fear. When your love grows weary, God's love grows stronger. When your resolve is weak, God's commitment is strong. Your decision to love your husband cannot be based on how you feel because your feelings of love and intimacy will fluctuate.

Loving your husband is an ongoing fulfillment of your wedding vows to stand by him when the going gets tough as well as when the going is easy.

While going through struggles is not your goal, coming out the other side is. Feelings of love should not be the center of your marriage—God should be at the center—but your decision to love your husband is the glue that will hold your marriage together for the long run.

worth thinking about

▶ **Chemical reactions** can fluctuate with your mood and the situation. Basing your feelings of love on your physical feelings can shortchange your relationship. Depend on your decision, not your feelings.

▶ **Keeping God** at the center of your marriage provides stability and security that cannot be shaken, no matter how big the storm.

▶ **Making the decision** to love your husband no matter how you feel will create stability in your marriage that goes beyond feelings.

> *I've never quit loving you and never will.*
> *Expect love, love, and more love!*
> Jeremiah 31:3, THE MESSAGE

Readers who enjoyed this book will also enjoy

100 Answers to 100 Questions About God

100 Answers to 100 Questions About God's Promises

100 Answers to 100 Questions About Loving Your Wife

100 Answers to 100 Questions About Prayer

100 Answers to 100 Questions to Ask Before You Say "I Do"